Patrick Lose's Whimsical Cross-Stitch

Patrick Lose's Whimsical Cross-Stitch

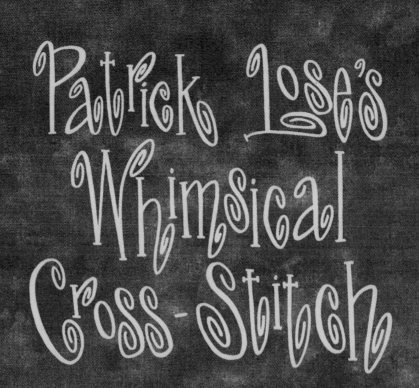

A Sterling/Chapelle Book
Sterling Publishing Co., Inc. New York

For Chapelle Limited

Owner: Jo Packham

Staff: Malissa Boatwright, Trice Boerens, Rebecca Christensen, Holly Fuller, Cherie Hanson, Holly Hollingsworth, Susan Jorgensen, Susan Laws, Amanda McPeck, Tammy Perkins, Jamie Pierce, Leslie Ridenour, Cindy Stoeckl, Nancy Whitley, and Lorrie Young.

Photography By: Ryne Hazen and Kevin Dilley for Hazen Photography: Cover and pgs. 22-23, 62-63, 68-69, 88-89, 112-113, 118-119, 126-127, 136-137. All others by Truitt Rogers for Truitt Photographics, Ft. Worth, TX.

The photographs in this book were taken at the homes of Robert and Donna Martin, Jim and Bonnie Graeber, and Jo Packham. Their cooperation, trust, and friendship is deeply appreciated.

Assistant to Patrick Lose: Lenny Houts

Models: Katie Lose, pgs. 30-31. Jodi Graeber, pgs. 44-45.

Library of Congress Cataloging-in-Publication Data

Lose, Patrick
    [Whimsical cross-stitch]
    Patrick Lose's Whimsical cross-stitch
      p.   cm.
    Includes index.
    ISBN 0-8069-1292-8
      1. Cross-stitch--Patterns. 2. Holiday decorations. I. Title: Whimsical cross-stitch.
TT778.C76L68 1995
746.44'3041--dc20
                       94-42099
                       CIP

10 9 8 7 6 5 4 3 2 1

A Sterling/Chapelle Book
Published by Sterling Publishing Company, Inc.
387 Park Avenue South, New York, N.Y. 10016
© 1995 by Chapelle Ltd.
Distributed in Canada by Sterling Publishing
c/o Canadian Manda Group, One Altantic Avenue, Suite 105
Toronto, Ontario, Canada M6K 3E7
Distributed in Great Britain and Europe by Cassell PLC
Villiers House, 41/47 Strand, London WC2N 5JE, England
Distributed in Australia by Capricorn (Australia) Pty Ltd.
P.O. Box 6651, Baulkham Hills, Business Centre, NSW 2153, Australia
Printed and Bound in China
All rights reserved

ISBN 0-8069-1292-8

For my daughter, Katie,
my greatest inspiration.

Chapter One

Table of

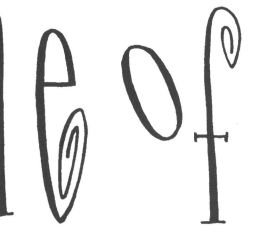

Chapter Two

Contents

Patrick Lose has spent his professional years in a variety of creative fields. He began his successful career as a costume designer for stage and screen. Costume credits include more than 50 productions and include work with celebrities such as Liza Minnelli and Jane Seymour.

An artist and illustrator since childhood, Patrick works in many mediums. When he sits down to "doodle" at the drawing board, he never knows what one of his designs might become. Whether it's a cross-stitch piece, wearable art, a greeting card, an ornament, or a piece of furniture, he enjoys creating it all.

His craft, clothing, and home decorating accessories have appeared frequently in such national magazines as *Better Homes and Gardens*, *Country Crafts*, *Christmas Ideas*, *Christmas Ornaments*, *Santa Claus*, *Decorative Woodcrafts*, *Craft and Wear*, *American Patchwork and Quilting*, and others. Publications featuring his designs have reached over 18 million subscribers.

Patrick also designs fabrics for United Notions and Fabrics, many of which were used to create the projects throughout this book and to decorate its pages.

Out on a Whim, Patrick Lose's company name, appropriately describes his original creations. Available in fabric and crafts stores nationwide, his patterns for making clothing, dolls, home decorating accessories, and holiday crafts feature folk-art whimsy with a contemporary twist.

All original illustrations by Patrick Lose. If you would like more information about Patrick's designs and **Out on a Whim** *patterns for wearable art, quilts, wood and holiday crafts, write to* **Out on a Whim,** *P.O. Box 451, Altoona, Iowa 50009.*

King
and Queen
of Hearts

Stitch Count: 45 x 68

16

King of Hearts

Sample

Stitched on white Aida 14, the finished design size is 3¼" x 4⅞". The fabric was cut 10" x 11".

Fabrics	Design Sizes
Aida 11	4⅛" x 6⅛"
Aida 18	2½" x 3¾"
Hardanger 22	2" x 3⅛"

	DMC		Anchor
	Cross-stitch (3 strands)		
□		White	1
▨	742	Tangerine lt.	303
▨	948	Peach vy. lt.	880
▨	818	Baby Pink	48
■	304	Christmas Red med.	47
■	550	Violet vy. dk.	101
■	796	Royal Blue dk.	133
■	400	Mahogany	351
▨	452	Shell Gray med.	399
	Backstitch		
		White (3 strands)	1
—	310	Black (1 strand)	403
	Long stitch		
—	742	Tangerine lt. (6 strands)	303
— ⟨	304	Christmas Red med (1 strand)	47
		Gold Metallic (1 strand)	

17

Stitch Count: 45 x 69

20

Queen of Hearts

Stitched on white Aida 14, the finished design size is 3¼" x 4⅞". The fabric was cut 10" x 11".

Fabrics / Design Sizes

Fabrics	Design Sizes
Aida 11	4⅛" x 6¼"
Aida 18	2½" x 3⅞"
Hardanger 22	2" x 3⅛"

DMC / Anchor

	DMC		Anchor
	Cross-stitch (3 strands)		
☐		White	1
▨	742	Tangerine lt.	303
▨	743	Yellow med.	297
▨	948	Peach vy. lt.	880
▤	818	Baby Pink	48
■	304	Christmas Red med.	47
■	550	Violet vy. dk.	101
■	796	Royal Blue dk.	133
▨	452	Shell Gray med.	399
	Backstitch		
—	310	Black (1 strand)	403
	Long stitch		
—	742	Tangerine lt. (4 strands)	303
‹	304	Christmas Red med. (1 strand)	47
		Gold Metallic (1 strand)	
—	796	Royal Blue dk.	133

Royal Reading

Stitch Count: 25 x 49

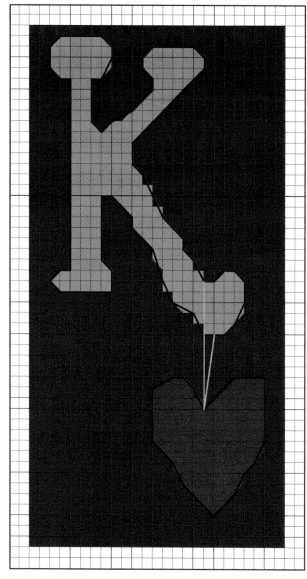

Stitch Count: 25 x 50

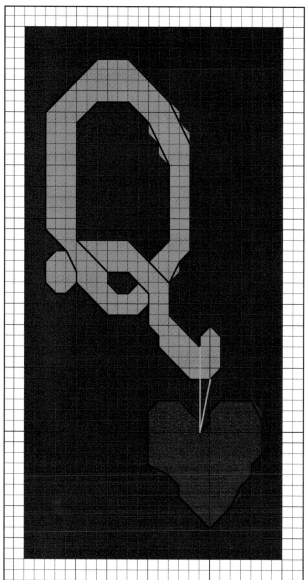

DMC
Anchor

Cross-stitch (3 strands)
- 743 Yellow med. (2 strands)   297
- 742 Tangerine lt. (1 strand)   303
- 321 Christmas Red   47
- 552 Violet dk. (1 strand)   99
- 550 Violet vy. dk. (2 strands)   101

Backstitch
- 310 Black (1 strand)   403

Long stitch
    Gold Metallic (2 strands)

24

Royal Reading

King

Sample

Stitched on clear perforated plastic 14, the finished design size is 1¾" x 3½". The plastic was cut 4" x 6".

Fabrics   Design Sizes

Aida 11   2¼" x 4½"
Aida 18   1⅜" x 2¾"
Hardanger 22   1⅛" x 2¼"

Queen

Sample

Stitched on clear perforated plastic 14, the finished design size is 1¾" x 3⅝". The plastic was cut 4" x 6".

Fabrics   Design Sizes

Aida 11   2¼" x 4½"
Aida 18   1⅜" x 2¾"
Hardanger 22   1⅛" x 2¼"

Materials

Finished designs on clear perforated plastic 14 trimmed with one square around design
Two 4½" x 2½" pieces of red Ultra Suede
Two 2½"-long red tassels
Two 1" lapel pins
Tacky glue

Directions

1. Trim Ultra Suede to ⅛" larger than finished design.

2. Glue design onto suede, placing tassel at center bottom between canvas and suede. Let dry completely.

3. Glue lapel pins to back about 1" from the top.

25

Have
a
Heart

Have a Heart

Stitch Count: 76 x 77

Sample

Stitched on royal blue Aida 14, the finished design size is 5½" x 5½". The fabric was cut 10" x 10".

Fabrics   Design Sizes

Aida 11	6⅞" x 7"
Aida 18	4¼" x 4¼"
Hardanger 22	3½" x 3½"

DMC   Anchor

Cross-stitch (3 strands)

	743	Yellow med.	297
	743	Yellow med. (2 strands)	297
	742	Tangerine lt. (1 strand)	303
	606	Orange Red br. (2 strands)	335
	666	Christmas Red br. (1 strand)	46
	321	Christmas Red (2 strands)	47
	304	Christmas Red med. (1 strand)	47
	797	Royal Blue (2 strands)	132
	820	Royal Blue vy. dk. (1 strand)	134
	986	Forest Green vy. dk.	246

Backstitch (2 strands)

—	310	Black	403

French Knots (1 strand Pearl Cotton #5)

•	743	Yellow med.	297

Materials

12" x 12" pillow form
Finished design on royal blue Aida 14 centered and trimmed to 8½" square
⅛ yard red print fabric
1 yard blue print fabric
Matching thread
1½ yards cording

Directions

All seams ⅜"

1. From blue fabric, cut four 36" x 6½" strips. Set aside for ruffle edge. Cut two 3½" x 8½" and two 3½" x 12¾" strips for pillow front. Cut 13½" square for back.

2. Place shorter blue strips on each side of design edges, right sides together. Sew seams. Fold fabric out and press. Place the longer strips along top and bottom of design. Sew seams, fold out, and press.

3. Cut one 34" x 1" strip of red fabric. Fold and press both long edges under ¼", making a 34" x ½" strip. Pin, centering over seam and mitering corners to form a frame around cross-stitch design. Top-stitch very close to edges.

4. Cut two 3" x 30" strips red fabric. With right sides together, sew one short edge together. Open seam and press. Place cording down center of wrong side of fabric. Fold fabric in half with cording inside. With zipper foot, stitch very close to cording to make piping. Pin around pillow front, rounding corners slightly, and sew into place.

5. Sew the blue fabric strips together at the short ends to make a large circle. Press in half with wrong sides together. Sew a gathering stitch along raw edge. Pull thread tightly. Pin to pillow front, adjusting gathers evenly. Sew into place.

6. Pin front and back of pillow, wrong sides together, keeping ruffle on the inside. Sew three sides together. Turn and insert pillow form. Whipstitch opening closed.

Whimsical Wearables

Whimsical Wearables

Button Covers

Sample

Stitched on royal blue Aida 14, the finished design size of each button is 1" x 1". The fabric was cut 9" x 9" (for all five).

Fabrics — Design Sizes

Fabrics	Design Sizes
Aida 11	1¼" x 1¼"
Aida 18	¾" x ¾"
Hardanger 22	⅝" x ⅝"

Materials

5 button covers
Five 1" squares of heavy cardboard
Finished designs on royal blue Aida 14 each
    trimmed and centered to 1¾" squares
3" square of blue Ultra Suede
Tacky glue

Directions

1. Center a cardboard square on the back of each design. Pull Aida around cardboard onto back and glue.

2. Cut Ultra Suede into 1" squares. Glue to backs of cardboard.

3. Center one button cover to back of each square and glue.

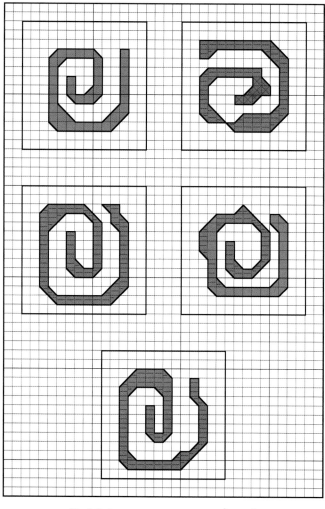

DMC — Anchor

	DMC		Anchor
Cross-stitch (3 strands)			
■	743	Yellow med.	297
■	743	Yellow med. (2 strands)	297
	742	Tangerine lt. (1 strand)	303
▨	742	Tangerine lt.	303
	Backstitch (2 strands)		
—	310	Black	403

32

Collar Swag

Sample

Stitched on white perforated plastic 14, the finished design size is 4⅝" x 1¾". The plastic was cut 7" x 4".

Fabrics  Design Sizes

Aida 11	5⅞" x 2¼"
Aida 18	3⅝" x 1⅜"
Hardanger 22	3" x 1⅛"

Materials

2 tie tacks
Finished design on white perforated plastic 14
    trimmed with one square around outside
3" x 6" piece of red Ultra Suede
Tacky glue

Directions

1. Trim Ultra Suede to ⅛" larger than finished design.

2. Glue design onto suede. Let dry completely.

3. Glue tie tacks to center back of each heart about ¾" from top.

DMC		Anchor
Cross-stitch (3 strands)		
743	Yellow med.	297
743	Yellow med. (2 strands)	297
742	Tangerine lt. (1 strand)	303
606	Orange Red br. (2 strands)	335
666	Christmas Red br. (1 strand)	46
321	Christmas Red (2 strands)	47
304	Christmas Red med. (1 strand)	47
986	Forest Green vy. dk.	246
Backstitch (2 strands)		
310	Black	403
Beads (Western Crafts)		
#145	size 10/0 Indian bead	
	33 Orange lt.	
#4996	Opaque "E" bead	
	22 Royal	

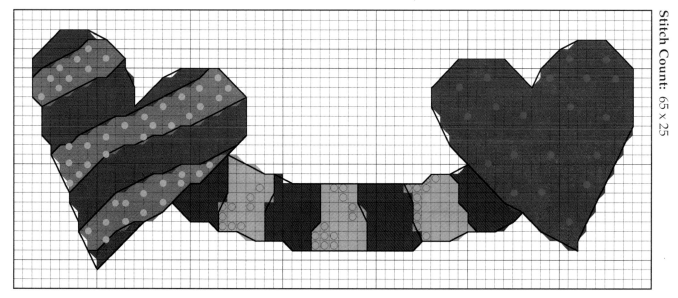

Stitch Count: 65 x 25

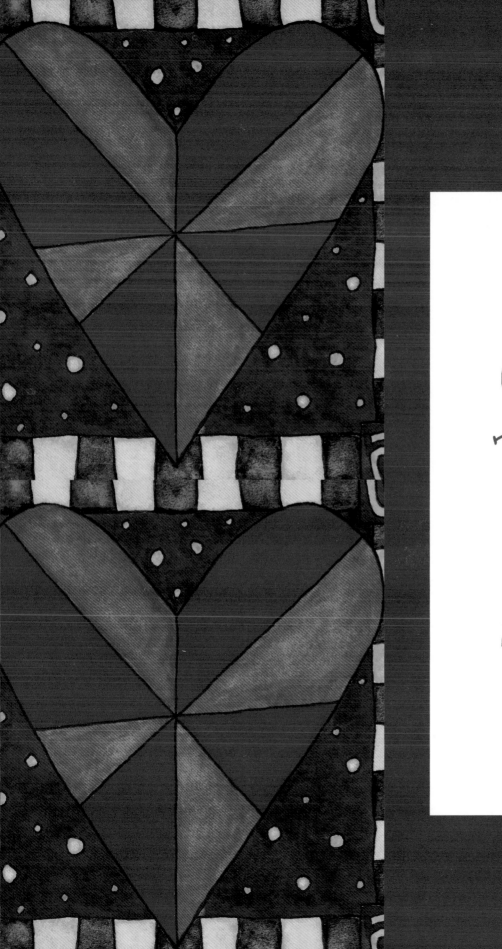

Lots
of
Love

Stitch Count: 36 x 36

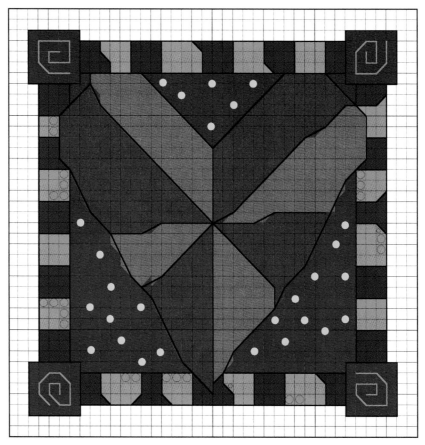

Lots of Love

Sample

Stitched on clear perforated plastic 14, the finished design size is 2⅝" x 2⅝". The plastic was cut 6" x 6".

Fabrics   Design Sizes

Fabrics	Design Sizes
Aida 11	3¼" x 3¼"
Aida 18	2" x 2"
Hardanger 22	1⅝" x 1⅝"

DMC   Anchor

Cross-stitch (3 strands)

	DMC		Anchor
	743	Yellow med.	297
	743	Yellow med. (2 strands)	297
	742	Tangerine lt. (1 strand)	303
	606	Orange Red br. (2 strands)	335
	666	Christmas Red br. (1 strand)	46
	321	Christmas Red (2 strands)	47
	304	Christmas Red med. (1 strand)	47
	797	Royal Blue (2 strands)	132
	820	Royal blue vy. dk. (1 strand)	246
	986	Forest Green vy. dk.	246

Backstitch (2 strands)

	DMC		Anchor
	743	Yellow med.	297
−	310	Black	403

Beads (Western Crafts)
#145 size 10/0 Indian beads
25 Yellow

Materials

One 1" lapel pin
3" gold charm chain
9 assorted charms
Finished design on clear perforated plastic 14
    trimmed with one square around outside
4" square of blue Ultra Suede
Tacky glue

Directions

1. Trim Ultra Suede to ⅛" larger than design.

2. Glue design onto suede and let dry completely.

3. Glue lapel pin to back about 1" from the top.

4. Tack chain to back bottom corners. Attach largest charm to center of chain and four charms on each side.

LOSE '94

37

Sweetheart Sachet

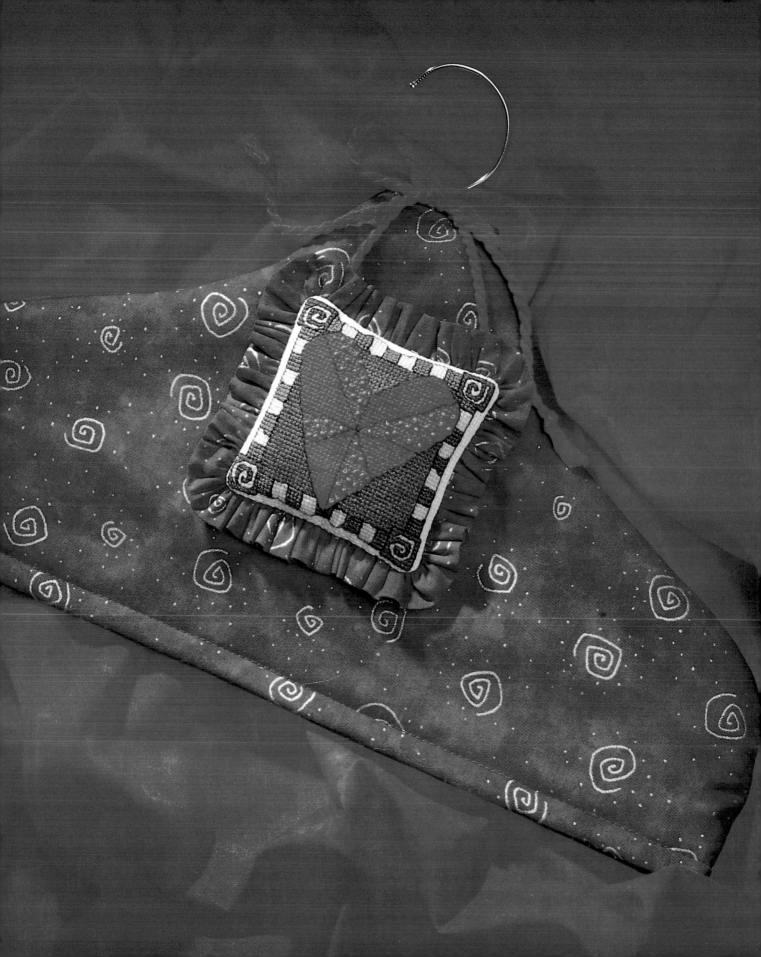

Sweetheart Sachet

Sample

Stitched on white Aida 14, the finished design size is 3⅝" x 3⅝". The fabric was cut 7" x 7".

Fabrics   Design Sizes

Aida 11   4⅝" x 4⅝"
Aida 18   2⅞" x 2⅞"
Hardanger 22   2⅜" x 2⅜"

Materials

Finished design on white Aida 14 centered and
    trimmed to 5" square
One 3" x 36" strip and one 5" square blue fabric
Matching thread
1 yard red cotton cording
1½ cups potpourri

Directions

1. For ruffle, sew short ends of fabric strip together, forming a large circle. Press in half wrong sides together. Sew a gathering stitch along raw edge. Pull thread tightly. Pin to sachet front, adjusting gathers evenly. Sew into place.

2. Cut red cording in half and tack one piece on each top side of sachet behind ruffle.

3. Place 5" fabric square, right side down, on sachet front. Sew around three sides, keeping ruffle and cording inside. Turn. Fill with pot-pourri and slip-stitch closed. Knot ends and tie bow in top of cording for hanger.

DMC   Anchor

Cross-stitch (3 strands)

	DMC		Anchor
	743	Yellow med.	297
	743	Yellow med. (2 strands)	297
	742	Tangerine lt. (1 strand)	303
	606	Orange Red br. (2 strands)	335
	666	Christmas Red br. (1 strand)	46
	321	Christmas Red (2 strands)	47
	304	Christmas Red med. (1 strand)	47
	797	Royal Blue (2 strands)	132
	820	Royal blue vy. dk. (1 strand)	246
	986	Forest Green vy. dk.	246

Backstitch (2 strands)
- 310 Black   403

Beads (Western Crafts)
- #145 size 10/0 Indian bead
    33 light orange

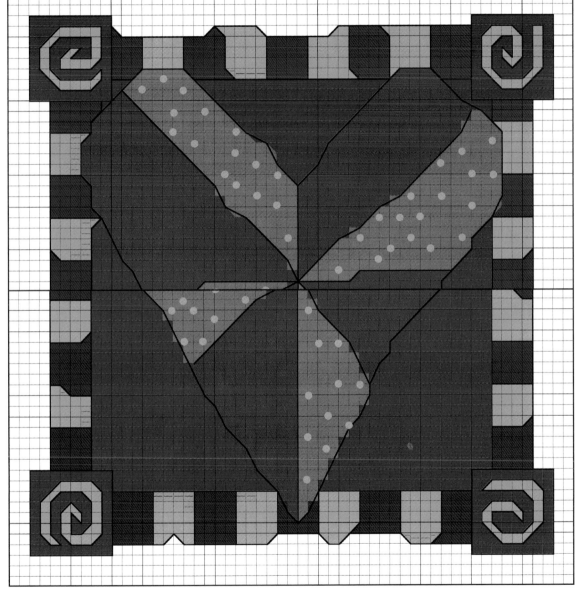

41

Chapter Two

Wearin'
o' the
green

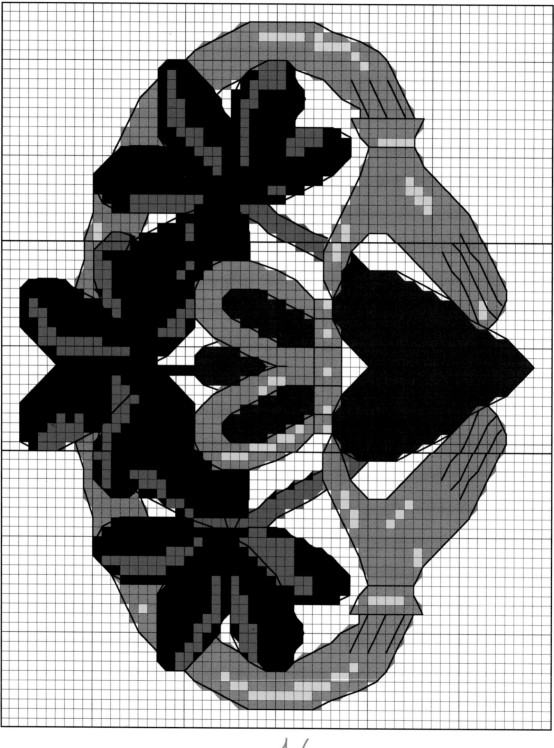

46

Wearin' o' the Green

Sample

Stitched on a stockinette sweater, the finished design size is 8⅛" x 6".

Fabrics	Design Sizes
Aida 11	6½" x 5⅛"
Aida 14	5⅛" x 4"
Aida 18	4" x 3⅛"
Hardanger 22	3¼" x 2½"

	DMC	Anchor
	Cross-stitch (3 strands)	
☐	726 Topaz lt.	295
▨	725 Topaz	306
■	321 Christmas Red	47
▨	367 Pistachio Green dk.	216
■	319 Pistachio Green vy. dk.	246
	Backstitch (2 strands)	
▬	310 Black	403

For a
Lovely Lass

Stitch Count: 40 x 32

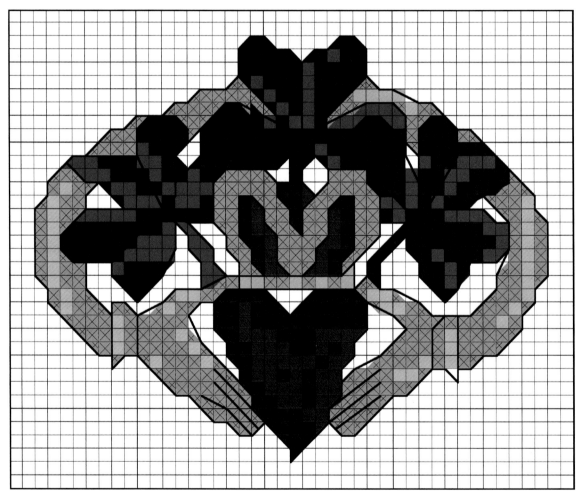

For a Lovely Lass

Sample

Stitched on antique white Cashel linen 28 over 2 threads, the finished design size is 2⅞" x 2¼". The fabric was cut 6" x 6".

Fabrics / Design Sizes

Fabrics	Design Sizes
Aida 11	3⅝" x 3"
Aida 18	2¼" x 1¾"
Hardanger 22	1⅞" x 1½"

DMC / Anchor

	DMC	Anchor
	Cross-stitch (2 strands)	
▨	726 Topaz lt.	295
⊠	725 Topaz	306
◼	321 Christmas Red	47
◼	498 Christmas Red dk.	20
◼	367 Pistachio Green dk.	216
◼	319 Pistachio Green vy. dk.	246
	Backstitch (1 strand)	
—	310 Black	403

Materials

Black oval porcelain box
Finished design on antique white Cashel linen 28 trimmed 1½" larger than box
Small amount of stuffing
Glue

Directions

1. Remove cardboard insert from box lid. Glue a mound of stuffing on top.

2. Make ¼" V-cuts around design edge. Place finished design on top of stuffing and wrap over to back. Glue.

3. Push cushioned design up through lid opening and glue into place.

Erin Go Bragh

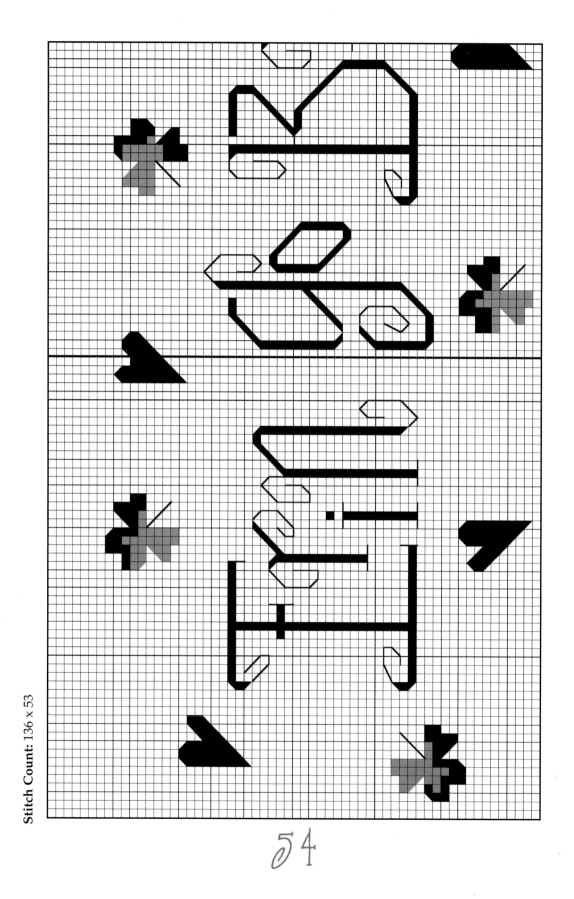

Stitch Count: 136 x 53

54

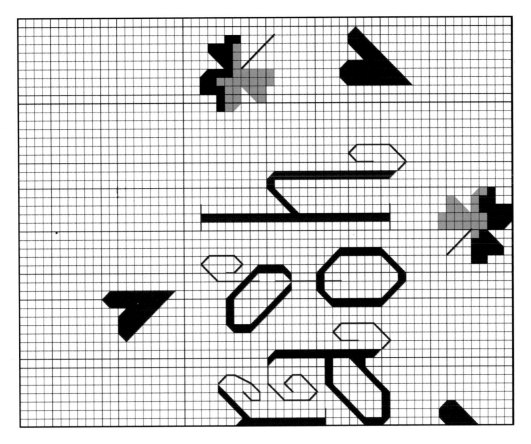

Erin Go Bragh

Sample

Stitched on cream bread cover 14 over 1 thread, the finished design size is 9¾" x 3¾". The fabric was cut 18" x 18".

Fabrics

Design Sizes

Aida 11   12⅜" x 4¾"
Aida 18   7½" x 3"
Hardanger 22   6⅛" x 2⅜"

DMC   Anchor

Cross-stitch (3 strands)
■ 321 Christmas Red   47
▨ ⟨ 367 Pistachio Green dk. (2 strands)   216
    319 Pistachio Green vy. dk. (1 strand)   246
■ 319 Pistachio Green vy. dk.   246

Backstitch (2 strands)
— 319 Pistachio Green vy. dk.   246

55

Luck
o' the
Irish

Stitch Count: 34 x 34

Luck o' the Irish

Sample

Stitched on a cream napkin 14 over 1 thread, the finished design size is 2⅜" x 2⅜". The fabric was cut 15" x 15".

Fabrics   Design Sizes

Aida 11   3⅛" x 3⅛"
Aida 18   1⅞" x 1⅞"
Hardanger 22   1½" x 1½"

DMC   Anchor

Cross-stitch (3 strands)
■ 367 Pistachio Green dk.   216
■ 319 Pistachio Green vy. dk.   246

The Claddagh

An old Irish legend tells of a fishing boat from the village of
Claddagh that was attacked by pirates. The fishermen were cap-
tured and taken as slaves. One young fisherman was to be married that very week. His bride-to-be was heartbroken. While a
slave, the young man became an expert goldsmith. He created a
unique ring for his true love with an image of a crowned heart
held by two hands. The heart symbolized their love, the crown
their loyalty, and the clasped hands their friendship. Years later,
he escaped his captors and returned to his village to find that his
love had never married. He presented her with the ring and they
were never separated again.

Jack-
in-the-
moon

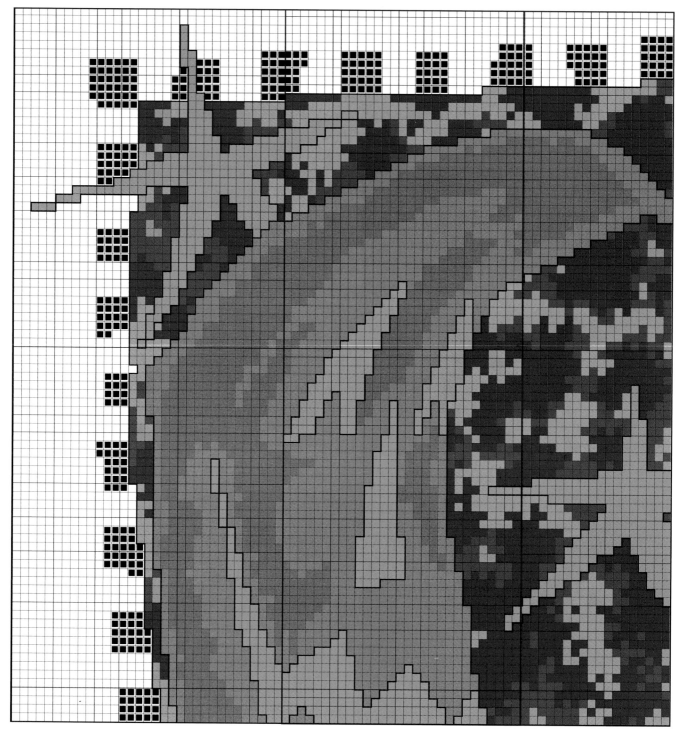

64

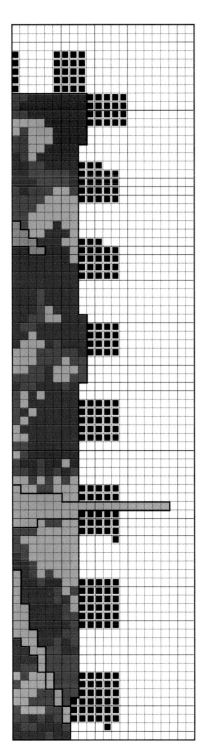

Jack-in-the-Moon

Sample

Stitched on black Heatherfield 26 over 2 threads, the finished design size is 7⅞" x 10". The fabric was cut 15" x 18".

Fabrics   Design Sizes

Aida 11   9⅜" x 11⅞"
Aida 14   7⅜" x 9¼"
Aida 18   5¾" x 7¼"
Hardanger 22   4⅝" x 5⅞"

DMC   Anchor

Cross-stitch (2 strands)
■		White	1
■	743	Yellow med.	297
■	947	Burnt Orange	330
■	720	Orange Spice dk.	326
■	209	Lavender dk.	105
■	552	Violet dk.	99
■	550	Violet vy. dk.	101

Backstitch (1 strand)
| — | 310 | Black | 403 |

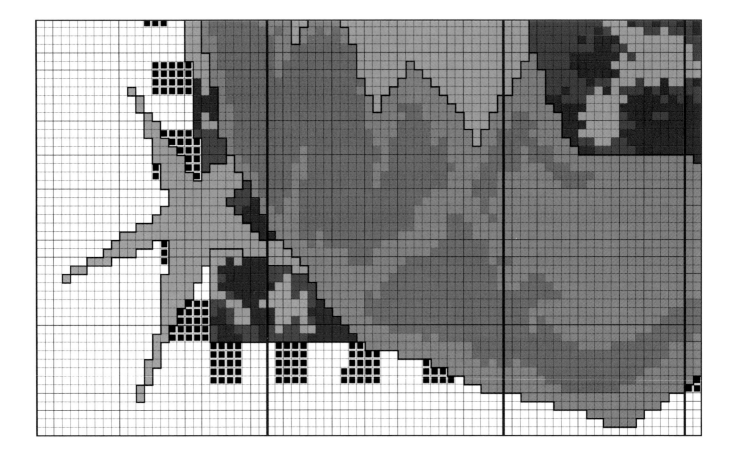

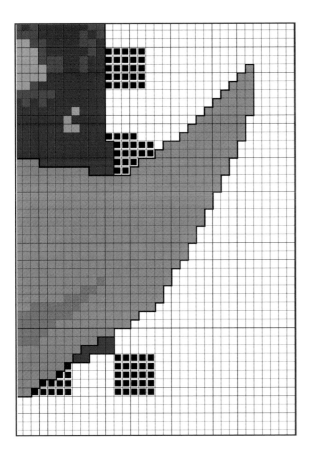

Materials

Finished design on black Heatherfield 26
    trimmed to 12" x 15"
One 12" x 15" piece, one 43" x 4" strip and
    two 15" x 4" strips black Heatherfield 26
½ yard colorful fabric for lining
½ yard iron-on heavyweight interfacing
Black thread

Directions

1. Press interfacing onto back side of design, 12" x 15" black fabric and 43" x 4" black strip. Zigzag edges.

2. Starting at top edge of design, sew 43" x 4" strip, right sides together, along sides and bottom of bag. Sew on back piece in the same manner.

3. From lining fabric, cut two 12" x 15" pieces and one 43" x 4" strip. Omitting interfacing, stitch lining together in same manner as bag, leaving a 5" opening in one bottom seam.

4. With right sides together, fold a 15" x 4" black strip in half lengthwise and sew around edges, leaving one end open. Turn, press and whipstitch opening closed. Repeat with other strip. These are the handles.

5. Baste handles to the inside of black bag on both top edges.

6. Place lining and bag with right sides together and pin around top edge. Sew around edge, making sure to backstitch over handles.

7. Turn bag right side out through the 5" opening in lining. Whipstitch closed. Stuff lining into bag and press.

Magnetic
Personalities

Magnetic Personalities

Stitch Count: 26 x 22

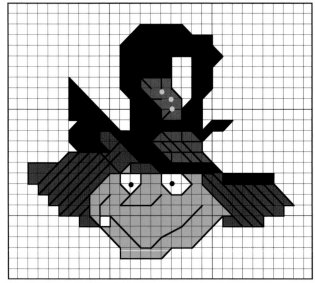

Sample

Stitched on white Aida 14, the finished design size is 1⅞" x 1⅝". The fabric was cut 4" x 4".

Fabrics	Design Sizes
Aida 11	2⅜" x 2"
Aida 18	1½" x 1¼"
Hardanger 22	1⅛" x 1"

Stitch Count: 27 x 36

Sample

Stitched on white Aida 14, the finished design size is 1⅞" x 2⅝". The fabric was cut 4" x 6".

Fabrics	Design Sizes
Aida 11	2½" x 3¼"
Aida 18	1½" x 2"
Hardanger 22	1¼" x 1⅝"

Stitch Count: 26 x 25

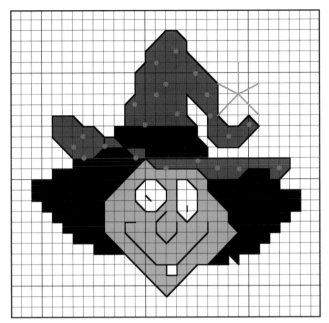

Sample

Stitched on white Aida 14, the finished design size is 1⅞" x 1¾". The fabric was cut 4" x 4".

Fabrics   Design Sizes

Aida 11	2⅜" x 2¼"
Aida 18	1½" x 1⅜"
Hardanger 22	1⅛" x 1⅛"

DMC   Anchor

Cross-Stitch (3 strands)

☐	White	1
■	947 Burnt Orange	330
■	553 Violet med.	98
■	704 Chartreuse br.	256
■	919 Red Copper	341
■	310 Black	403

Backstitch (1 strand)

—	310 Black	403

Long Stitch (2 strands)

—	742 Tangerine lt.	303

French Knots (1 strand)

·	742 Tangerine lt.	303
•	310 Black	403

Materials

3 magnets
Finished designs on white Aida 14, trimmed
    leaving one square around design
One each 3½" x 3" red, orange, purple Ultra
    Suede
Tacky glue

Directions

1. Trim the Ultra Suede ⅛" larger than the designs. Glue designs onto suede. (Gluing all the way to edge prevents Aida from fraying.) Let dry completely.

2. Glue magnets to back of witches.

71

Halloween
Hand
Towels

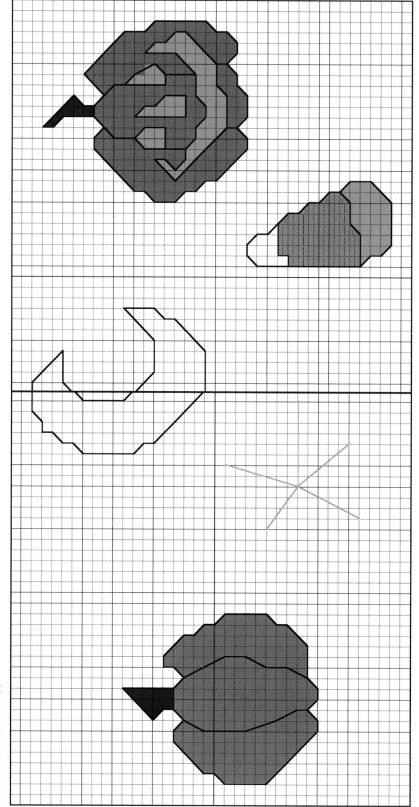

Halloween Hand Towels

Sample

Stitched on a black or white cross-stitch estate towel 14 over 1 thread, the finished design size is 5⅛" x 2½".

Fabrics  Design Sizes

Fabrics	Design Sizes
Aida 11	6½" x 3⅛"
Aida 18	4" x 2"
Hardanger 22	3¼" x 1⅝"

DMC	Anchor

Cross-stitch (3 strands)

			Anchor
☐		White	1
▣	973	Canary br.	290
▨	741	Tangerine med.	304
▨	741	Tangerine med. (2 strands)	304
	608	Orange Red (1 strand)	333
■	699	Christmas Green	923

Backstitch (1 strand)

—	310	Black	403

Long Stitch (3 strands)

–	973	Canary br.	290

Tricks
for
Treats

Stitch Count: 38 x 37

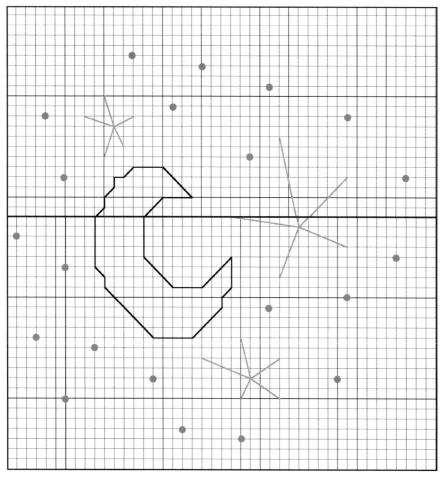

DMC   Anchor

Cross-stitch (3 strands)
☐   White   1

Backstitch (1 strand)
—   310 Black   403

Long Stitch (2 strands)
—   743 Yellow med.   297

Beads
●   #145 size 10/0 Indian beads
      33 orange lt.

Moon and Stars

Sample

Stitched on black Aida 14, the finished design size is 2¾" x 2⅝". The fabric was cut 6" x 6".

Fabrics   Design Sizes

Aida 11   3½" x 3⅜"
Aida 18   2⅛" x 2"
Hardanger 22   1¾" x 1⅝"

Candy Corn

Sample

Stitched on black Aida 14, the finished design size is 2½" x 2⅞". The fabric was cut 6" x 6".

Fabrics   Design Sizes

Aida 11   3⅛" x 3¾"
Aida 18   2" x 2¼"
Hardanger 22   1⅝" x 1⅞"

Tricks for Treats

Stitch Count: 35 x 41

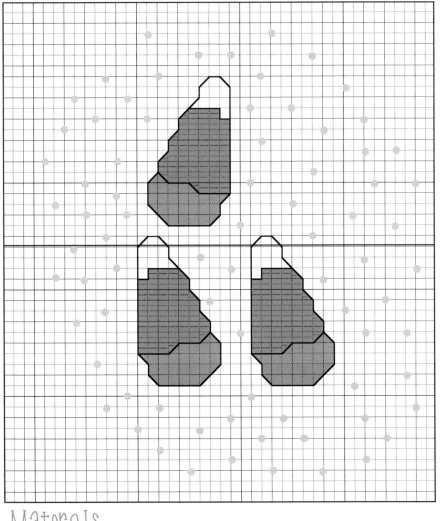

DMC   Anchor

Cross-stitch (3 strands)
☐   White   1
▨ 743 Yellow med.   297
▨ 741 Tangerine med.   304

Backstitch (1 strand)
— 310 Black   403

Beads
•   #145 size 10/0 Indian beads
         25 Yellow

Directions

1. Glue trimmed designs to the inside of jar rings with right side showing through top. Do not pull tight.

2. Pin bias tape around edge of fabric circle. Place ricrac under edge just enough to be stitched. Stitch.

3. Gathering slightly, glue fabric circle (right side up) to bottom of lid jar. Place batting circle on top of lid and glue to inside of ring.

4. Fill jar with candy and replace lid.

5. Tie remaining ricrac in a bow around lids. Glue to secure.

Materials

2 canning jars with lid and ring
Candy
Finished designs on black Aida 14 trimmed to
      3½" circles
Two 6½" fabric circles
Two 3" circles of batting
Matching thread
3 yards narrow black ricrac trim
1½ yards gold double-fold bias tape
Glue

Festive for Fall

Festive for Fall

Stitch Count: 16 x 19

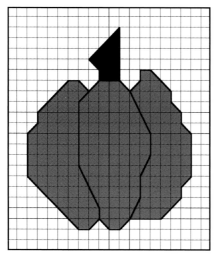

DMC		Anchor
Cross-stitch (3 strands)		
◼ 973 Canary br. (2 strands)		290
608 Orange Red (1 strand)		333
◼ 699 Christmas Green		923
Backstitch (2 strands)		
— 310 Black		403

Materials

Finished design on black perforated plastic 14
    trimmed with one square around outside
One 4" x 8" piece green Ultra Suede
Orange and gold raffia
Tacky glue

Directions

1. Trim Ultra Suede to ⅛" larger than design.

2. Glue design onto suede and let dry completely.

3. Center raffia on suede. Glue.

4. Tie raffia around candle and arrange.

Sample

Stitched on black perforated plastic 14, the finished design size is 1⅛" x 1⅜". The plastic was cut 5" x 5".

Fabrics   Design Sizes

Fabrics	Design Sizes
Aida 11	1½" x 1¾"
Aida 18	⅞" x 1"
Hardanger 22	¾" x ⅞"

Wacky
Witch

86

Wacky Witch

Sample

Stitched on white Aida 14, the finished design size is 4⅝" x 4⅛". The fabric was cut 7" x 7".

Fabrics   Design Sizes

Aida 11   5⅞" x 5¼"
Aida 18   3⅝" x 3¼"
Hardanger 22   3" x 2⅝"

DMC   Anchor

Cross-stitch (3 strands)
☐   White   1
■ 553 Violet med.   98
▨ 704 Chartreuse br.   256
■ 919 Red Copper   341
■ 310 Black   403

Backstitch (1 strand)
— 310 Black   403

French Knots (1 strand)
    742 Tangerine lt.   303
●   310 Black   403

Materials

Finished designs on white Aida trimmed
        leaving one square around design
One 6" x 5 ½" purple piece Ultra Suede
20" of ¼" wide purple satin ribbon
20" of ⅛" black satin ribbon
Tacky glue

Directions

1. Trim the Ultra Suede ⅛" larger than the designs. Glue designs onto suede. (Gluing all the way to edge prevents Aida from fraying.) Let dry completely.

2. Fold purple and black ribbons in half together. Tie a bow and glue tails to center back of witch for hanger.

Jolly Jack
-o-
lantern

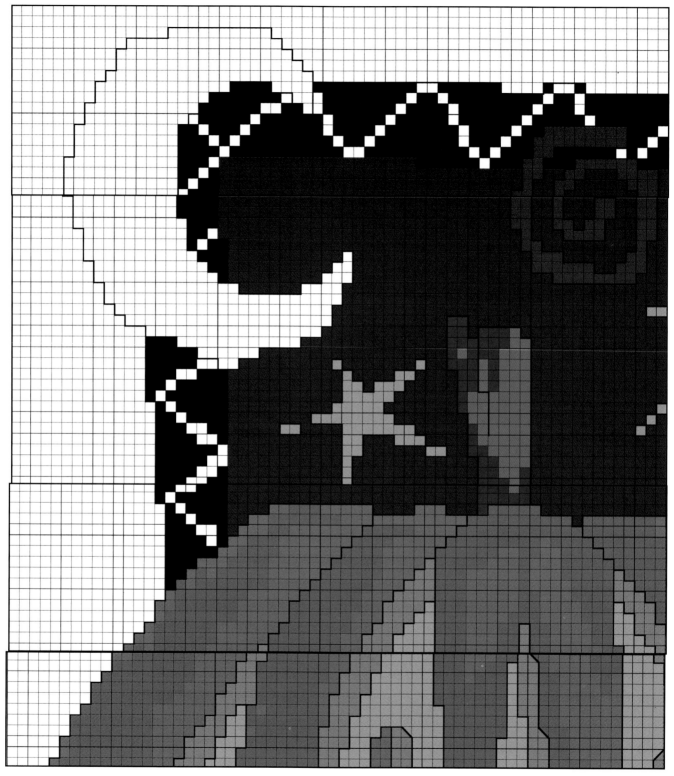

90

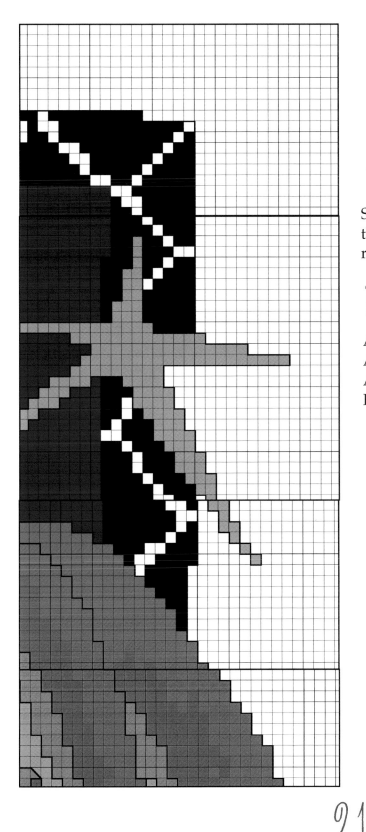

Jolly Jack-o-lantern

Sample

Stitched on Barnwood linen 32 over 2 threads, the finished design size is 5¾" x 8¾". The fabric was cut 9" x 15".

Fabrics / Design Sizes

Fabrics	Design Sizes
Aida 11	8¼" x 12⅝"
Aida 14	6½" x 9⅞"
Aida 18	5" x 7¾"
Hardanger 22	4⅛" x 6⅜"

DMC / Anchor

Cross-stitch (2 strands)

			Anchor
		White	1
	742	Tangerine lt.	303
	3825	Pale Pumpkin	323
	721	Orange Spice med.	324
	947	Burnt Orange	330
	321	Christmas Red	47
	550	Violet vy. dk.	101
	905	Parrot Green dk.	258
	909	Emerald Green vy. dk.	229
	310	Black	403

Backstitch (1 strand)
–	310	Black	403

91

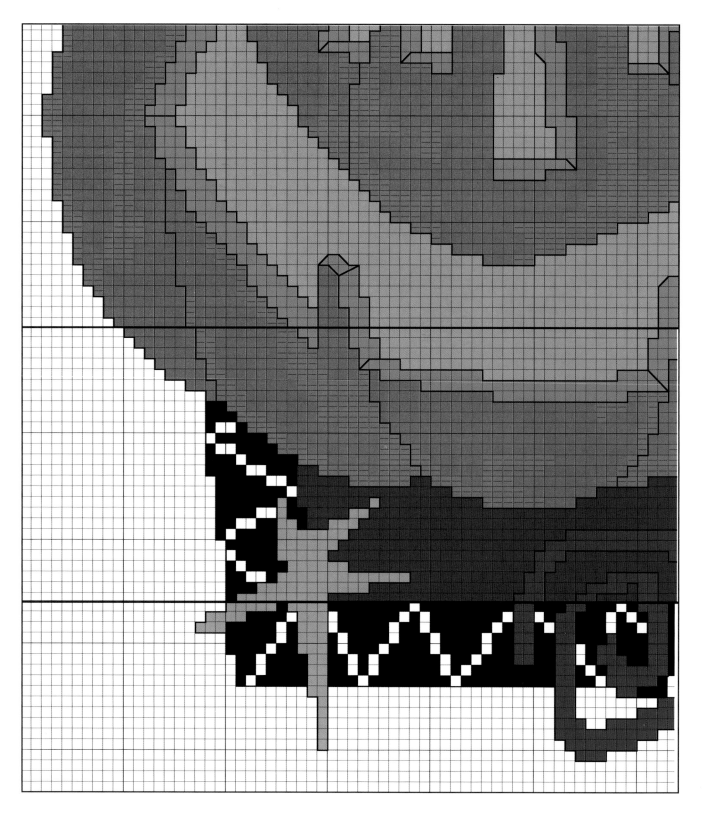

92

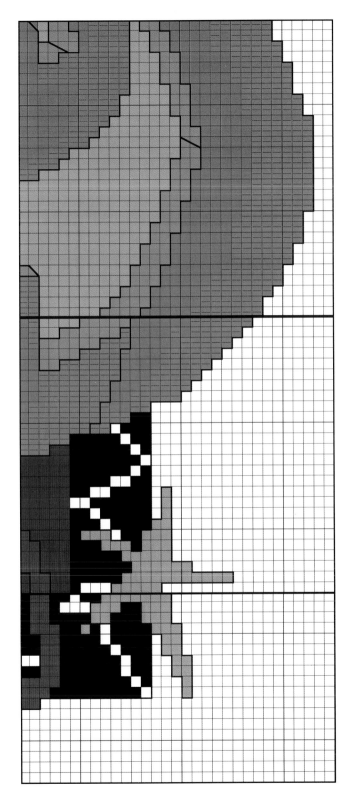

Jolly Jack-o-lantern
Banner Pattern

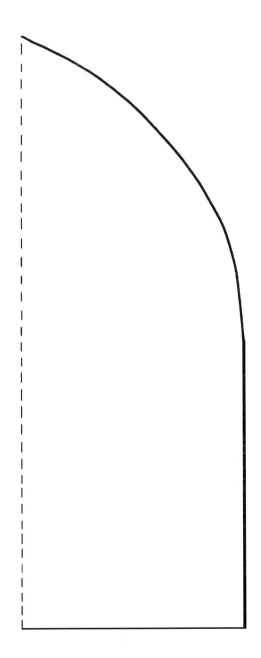

93

Jolly Jack-o-lantern Banner

Materials

Finished design on Barnwood linen 32
½ yard gold fabric
½ yard striped fabric
Scraps of red, purple and gold fabric for hanging stars, moon and swirls
½ yard iron-on interfacing
½ yard batting
Matching thread
Metallic gold thread
18" of ⅝"-wide purple ribbon
Fabric stiffener
Metallic gold spray paint
Metallic gold puff paint pen
Gold glitter spray
Tracing paper

Directions

All seams ½"

1. Photocopy pattern found on page 93 to 200 percent (pattern is half of original size). Transfer pattern to tracing paper, making sure to fold along dotted line.

2. Place pattern over center of cross-stitch design. Pin and cut out. Cut interfacing to pattern size and press onto back of finished cross-stitch. Sew a basting stitch ½" in from the edge around piece. Clip curves and press all edges under.

3. From gold fabric, cut 2 pieces 1½" larger on all sides than cross-stitch piece. Iron interfacing on the back of one of these pieces.

4. Center stitched piece on the front of gold interfaced fabric and pin in place. Using gold thread, stitch a decorative machine stitch around edge of design. Note: You could use a hand-embroidery blanket stitch if you prefer.

5. Cut 2 layers of batting to match backing. Layer as follows: gold back of banner, wrong side up, 2 layers of batting and banner front, right side up. Pin together. Sewing through all layers, stitch around design just outside of your decorative stitch. Baste around edges about ¼" inside.

6. For binding, cut striped fabric into a strip 3" x 45". Press in half lengthwise and then press into thirds. Starting at the front top side, sew, right sides together, down to bottom point. Trim. Fold over to back and hand-stitch closed. Repeat with other side, folding bottom point over to back. Bind top edge.

7. Cut purple ribbon into 3 even pieces. Fold each in half and baste to back of banner at top sides and center.

8. Find a whimsical stick and paint with gold spray paint. Let dry. Slide through ribbon loops. With gold thread, make a hanger at top of stick.

9. For hanging shapes, dip fabric scraps into fabric stiffener, following manufacturer's instructions. When dry, cut into desired shapes and paint edges with gold puff paint. Let dry. Use various lengths of gold thread to attach to banner and stick.

10. Lightly spray finished piece with gold glitter spray.

Chapter Four

Countdown
to
Christmas

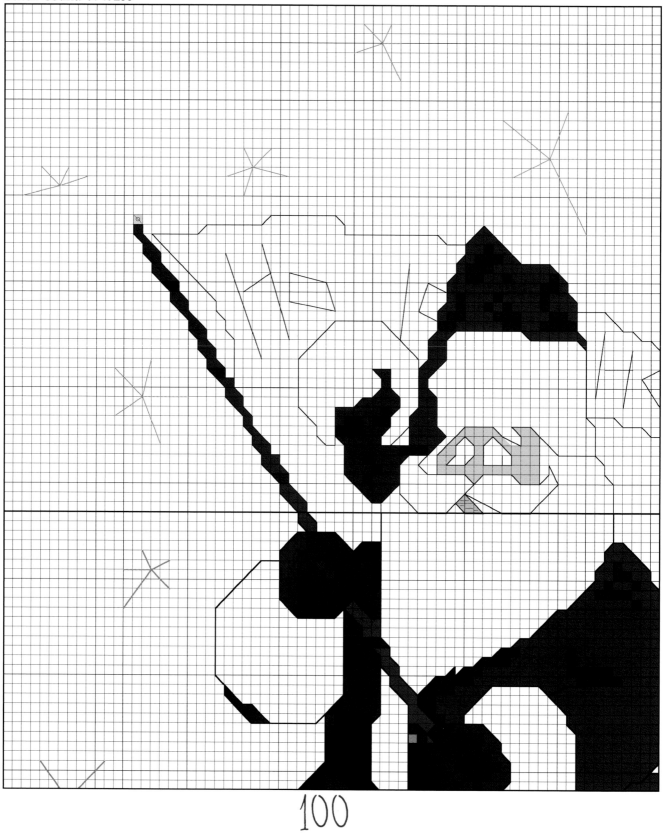

100

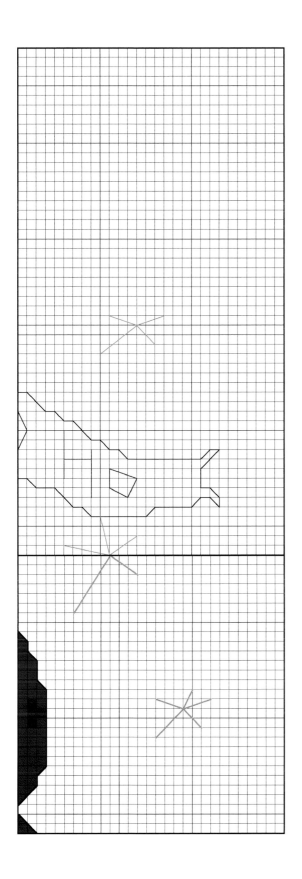

Countdown to Christmas

Sample

Stitched on white Aida 14, the finished design size is 6⅞" x 20⅜". The fabric was cut 11" x 24".

Fabrics   Design Sizes

Fabrics	Design Sizes
Aida 11	8⅞" x 26"
Aida 18	5⅜" x 15⅞"
Hardanger 22	4⅜" x 13"

	DMC		Anchor
	Cross-Stitch (3 strands)		
☐		White	1
▨	742	Tangerine lt.	303
▨	948	Peach vy. lt.	880
▨	3713	Salmon vy. lt.	271
■	321	Christmas Red	47
■	498	Christmas Red dk.	20
■	986	Forest Green vy. dk.	246
■	3345	Hunter Green dk.	398
■	433	Brown med.	371
■	310	Black	403
	Backstitch		
—	310	Black (3 strands)	403
	Long Stitch		
—	742	Tangerine lt.	303
—	986	Forest Green vy. dk.	246

101

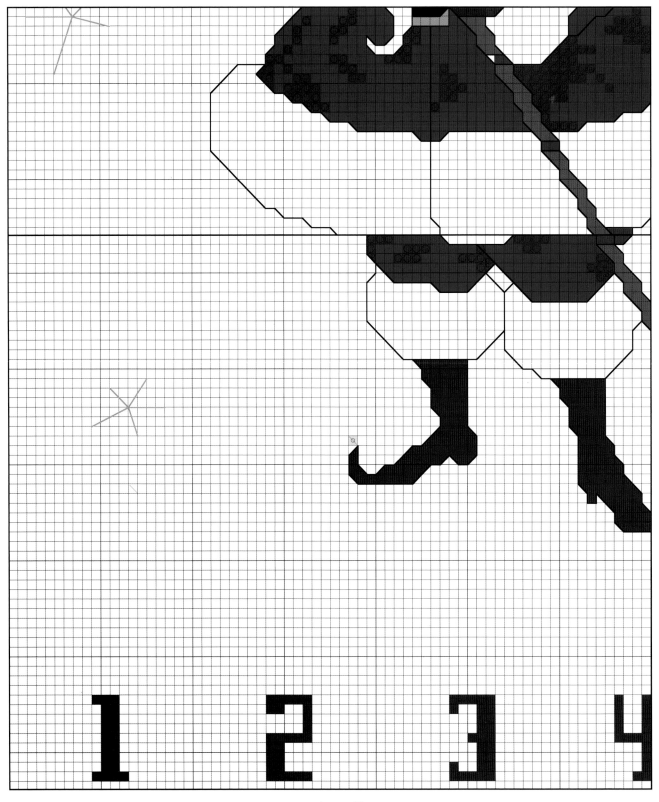

1 2 3 4

102

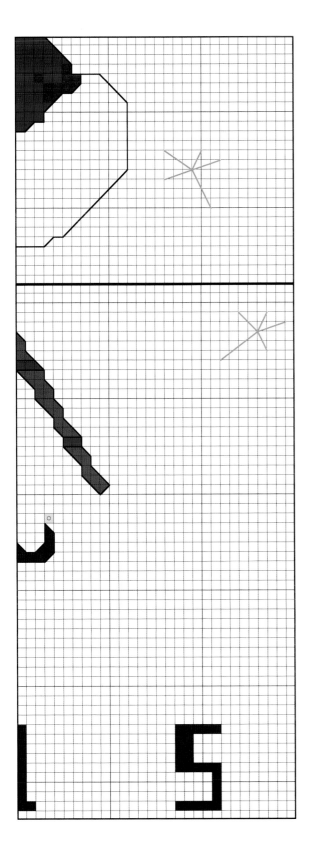

Countdown to Christmas Calendar

Materials

Finished design on white Aida 14 trimmed to fit pattern
15" x 30" green fabric for back
⅓ yard green fabric for front
⅛ yard red-and-green print fabric for binding
15" x 30" batting
6 yards of ⅛" wide red satin ribbon
Thread: red and invisible
Large-eyed needle
3 small brass bells
3½" green tassel
25 pieces hard candy
Tracing paper

Directions

All seams ¼" unless noted.

1. Using the diagram on page 105 as a guide, create a pattern for back piece on tracing paper. From back pattern, cut one piece from green fabric and one batting piece.

2. From ⅓ yard green fabric, cut five pattern pieces: one for front, using patterns on pages 106 and 107 for bottom and sides, and one 13¼" x 3" rectangle. Place bottom pieces right sides together and sew center seam on a diagonal.

Instructions continued on page 105.

103

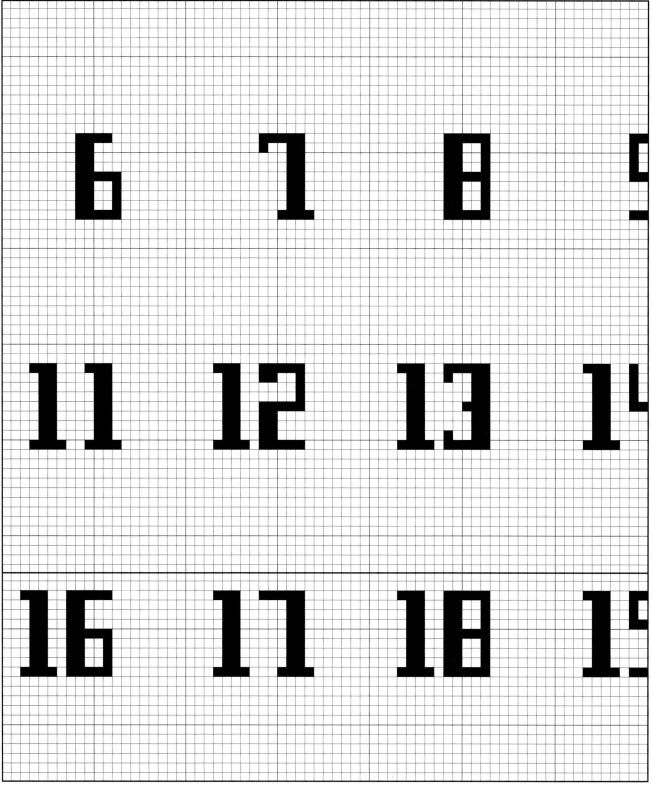

6 7 8 9

11 12 13 14

16 17 18 19

104

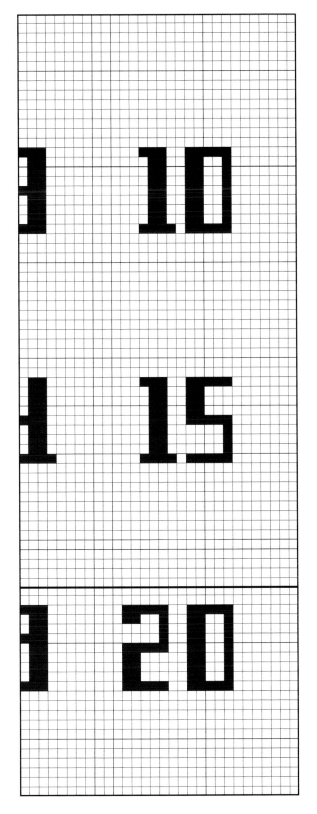

Instructions countinued from page 103.

Press open so that you have a V-shape. Sew side pieces onto the bottom piece. Place on cross-stitch design, right sides together, and pin fabric edge to Aida edge. Sew around sides and bottom. Sew top strip on.

3. Lay fabric back wrong side up and place batting piece on top. Lay design on top of batting. Pin all 3 layers. Sew with invisible thread along seams for quilted look.

4. Cut binding fabric into two 2" strips. Sew together, creating one long strip. Press long edges under ¼", fold in half lengthwise and press again. Open and place right sides together on front of calendar, starting at bottom center point. Sew around edges, mitering corners. Fold around to back side and whipstitch around back edge.

5. Tack bells onto boots and pole. Cut 25 strips of red satin ribbon into 9" lengths. Thread each ribbon through needle and sew above center of each number. Tie a piece of candy with a bow on each day. Tack tassel to bottom point.

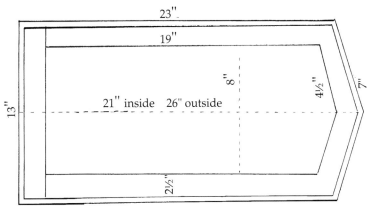

105

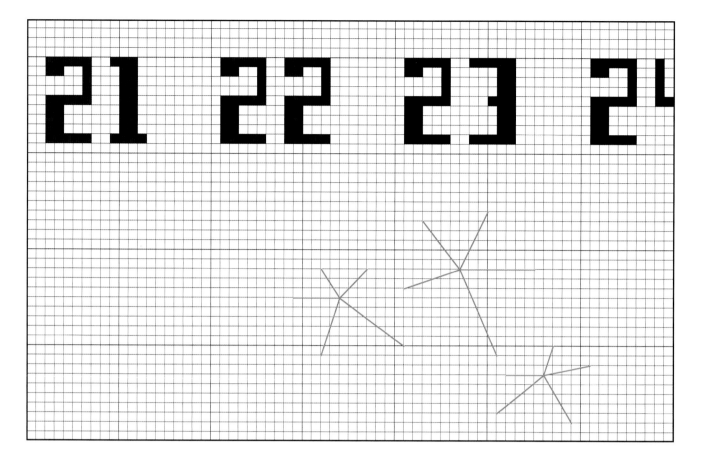

Side Border Cut 2.
20" x 24"

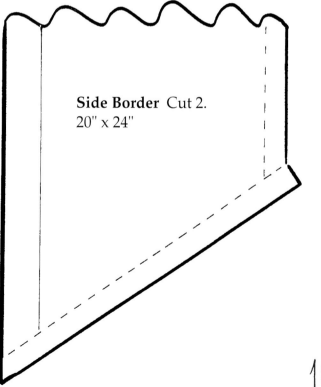

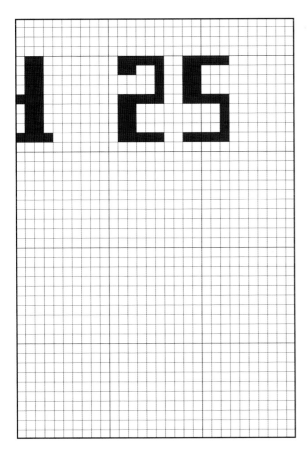

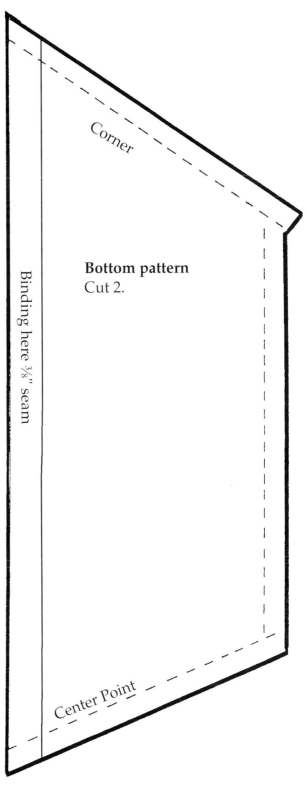

Corner

Binding here ⅜" seam

Bottom pattern
Cut 2.

Center Point

107

Let it Snow!

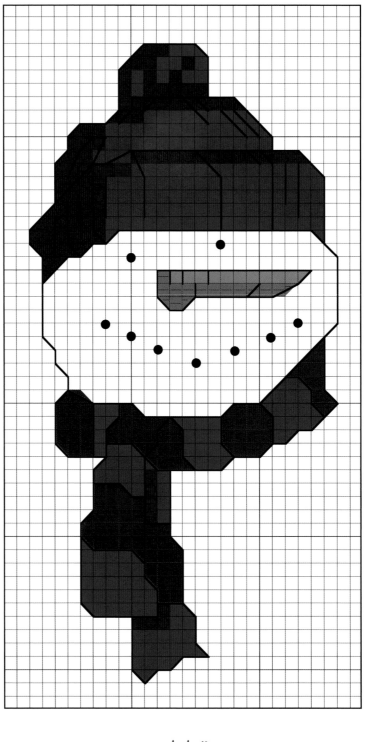

110

Let it Snow!

Sample

Stitched on clear perforated plastic 14, the finished design size is 1¾" x 3⅜". The plastic was cut 6" x 6".

Fabrics   Design Sizes

Aida 11	2⅛" x 4⅜"
Aida 18	1⅜" x 2⅝"
Hardanger 22	1⅛" x 2⅛"

DMC   Anchor

	Cross-stitch (3 strands)	
☐	White	1
▨	741 Tangerine-med.	741
▨	740 Tangerine	304
■	321 Christmas Red	47
■	700 Christmas Green br.	229
■	699 Christmas Green	923

	Backstitch (2 strands)	
—	310 Black	403

Beads
- #4996 Opaque E Beads
      2 Black

Materials

1" lapel pin
Finished design on clear perforated plastic 14 trimmed leaving one square around edge of design
3" x 5" green Ultra Suede
Matching thread
Tacky glue

Directions

1. Sew black beads onto snowman for eyes and mouth.

2. Trim Ultra Suede ⅛" larger than design.

3. Glue design onto suede. Let dry completely.

4. Glue lapel pin to back about 1" from top.

Folk Heart Frosty

Front Stitch Count: 41 x 72

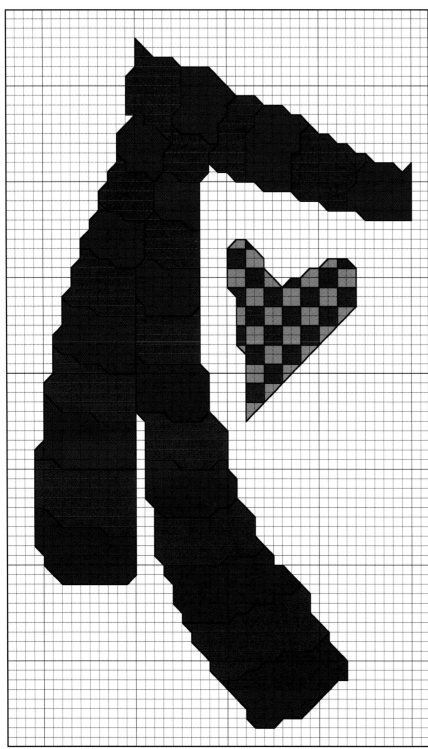

Folk Heart Frosty

Sample

Stitched on white Aida 14, the finished design size is 2⅞" x 5⅛" for the front and 2⅛" x 1¼" for the back. The fabric was cut 10" x 14" for each side.

Fabrics Design Sizes

Front:
Aida 11	3¾" x 6½"
Aida 18	2¼" x 4"
Hardanger 22	1⅞" x 3¼"

Back:
Aida 11	2¾" x 1⅝"
Aida 18	1⅝" x 1"
Hardanger 22	1⅜" x ⅞"

DMC   Anchor

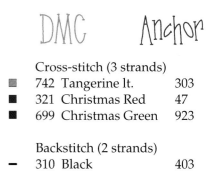

Cross-stitch (3 strands)
▨	742	Tangerine lt.	303
■	321	Christmas Red	47
■	699	Christmas Green	923

Backstitch (2 strands)
—	310	Black	403

114

742 Tangerine lt.

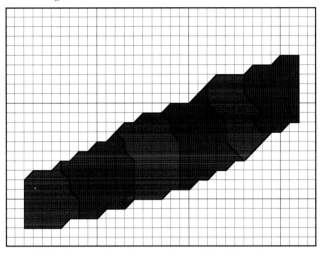

Materials

2 twigs, approximately 6" for arms
3" x 4" heavy cardboard for base
Orange and black sculpting clay (or you may
     paint clay)
Stuffing
Finished design on white Aida 14 (front and
     back)
3" x 4" white craft felt
Hot glue gun and glue sticks
Tracing paper

Directions

1. Photocopy snowman pattern at 200 percent (pattern is ½ original size.) Trace snowman pattern on tracing paper. Place pattern right side up on front piece of Aida and cut. Place pattern right side down on back piece of Aida and cut. With right sides together, sew a ¼" seam around leaving bottom open. Make sure to match cross-stitched scarf on both sides.

2. Turn and stuff firmly leaving ¾" unstuffed at bottom. Trace oval pattern on tracing paper and cut out. Place oval pattern piece on top of cardboard and trace. Cut out oval and place it ¾" into the bottom opening of the snowman, pushing the stuffing up firmly. Around the remaining ¾" at the bottom opening, make ⅝" clips, about an inch apart. Glue the opening closed by easing the bottom and gluing it to the cardboard base. Using the oval pattern, cut one from white felt and glue over th base to hide the raw edges.

3. With black sculpting clay, make seven ¼" pieces of coal for eyes and mouth. Form a carrot with the orange clay. Set clay according to package directions. Glue carrot, eyes and mouth onto snowman to make a face.

4. Cut two small holes in Aida to insert arms (see pattern). Carefully push arms in. Remove arms and place a small dot of glue in holes. Push arms back in and let dry.

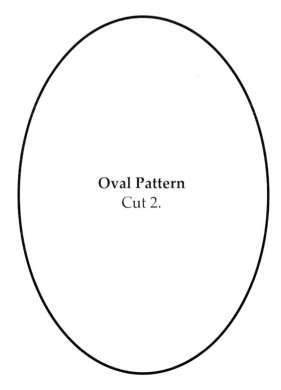

Oval Pattern
Cut 2.

Folk Heart Frosty Pattern

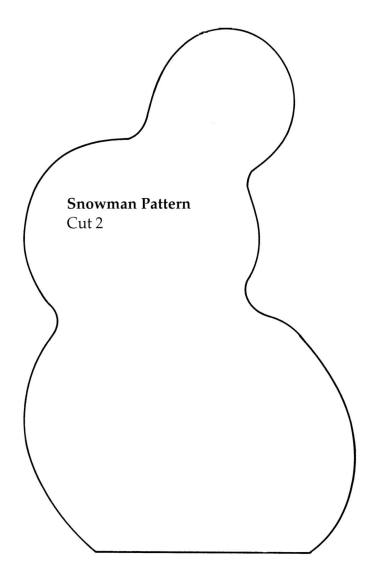

Snowman Pattern
Cut 2

116

Nuts About Christmas

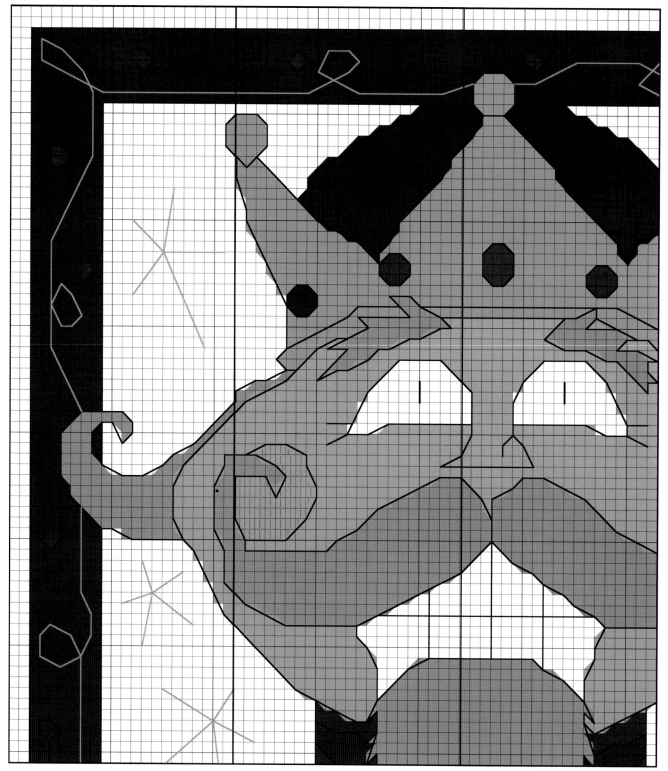

120

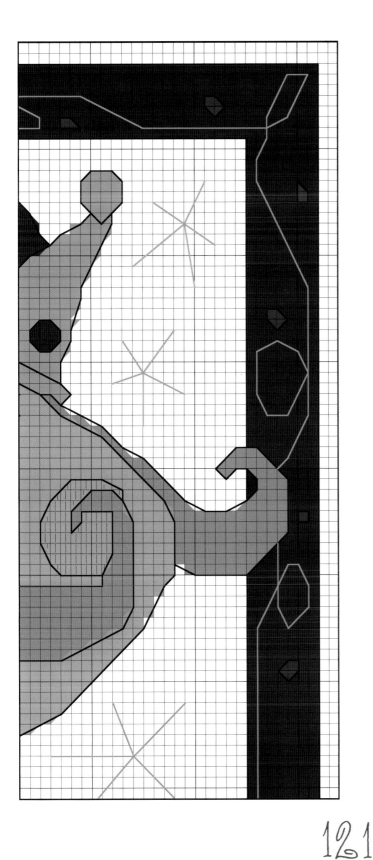

Nuts About Christmas

Sample

Stitched on royal blue Aida 14, the finished design size is 6⅜" x 8½". The fabric was cut 13" x 15".

Fabrics   Design Sizes

Aida 11   8⅛" x 10⅞"
Aida 18   5" x 6⅝"
Hardanger 22   4⅛" x 5⅜"

	DMC		Anchor
		Cross-stitch (3 strands)	
☐		White	1
▨	742	Tangerine lt.	303
▨	945	Peach Beige	881
▨	353	Peach	8
■	304	Christmas Red med.	47
■	796	Royal Blue dk.	133
■	3345	Hunter Green dk.	268
▨	415	Pearl Gray	398
		Backstitch	
=	742	Tangerine lt. (2 strands)	303
—	310	Black (3 strands)	403
		Long Stitch	
—	742	Tangerine lt.	303

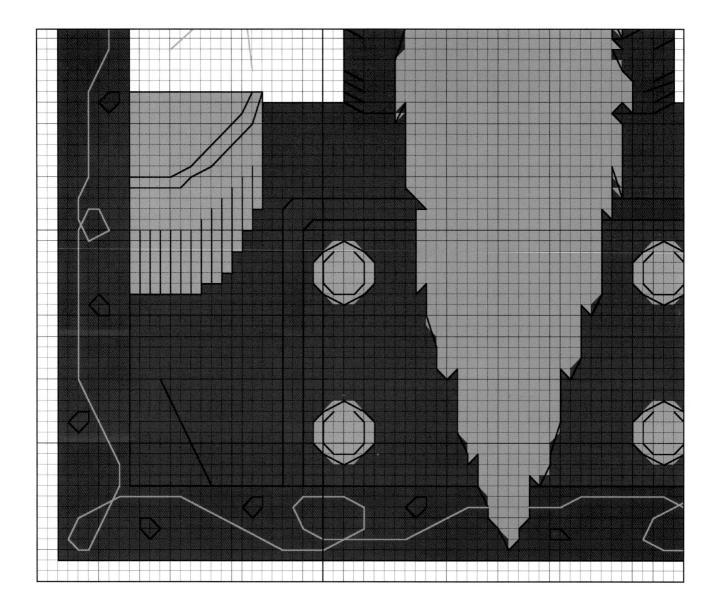

122

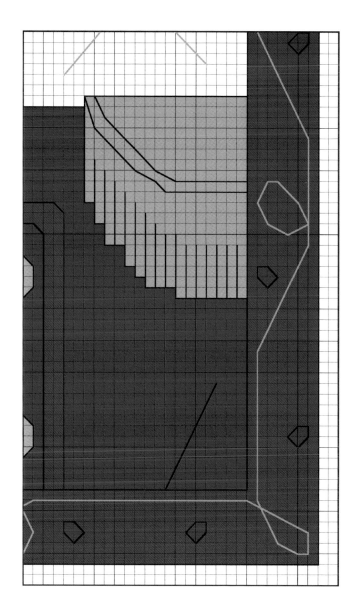

123

Joyride

Joyride

Stitch Count: 126 x 128

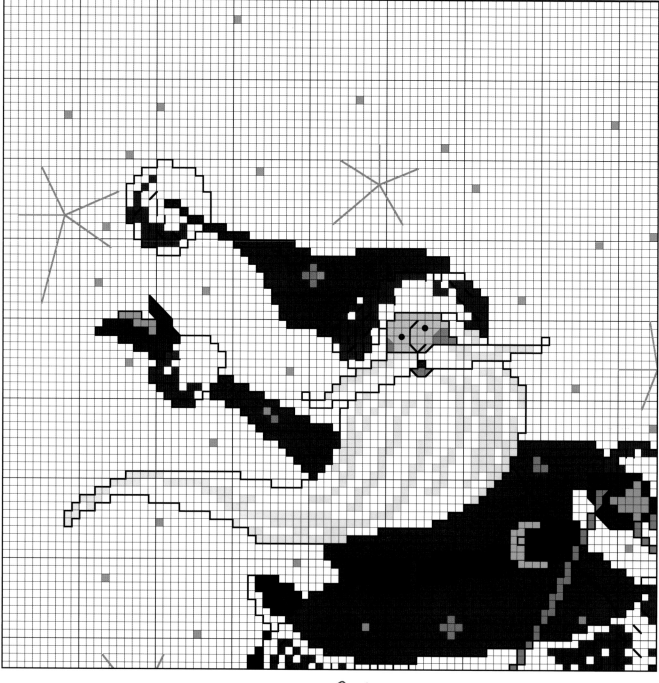

126

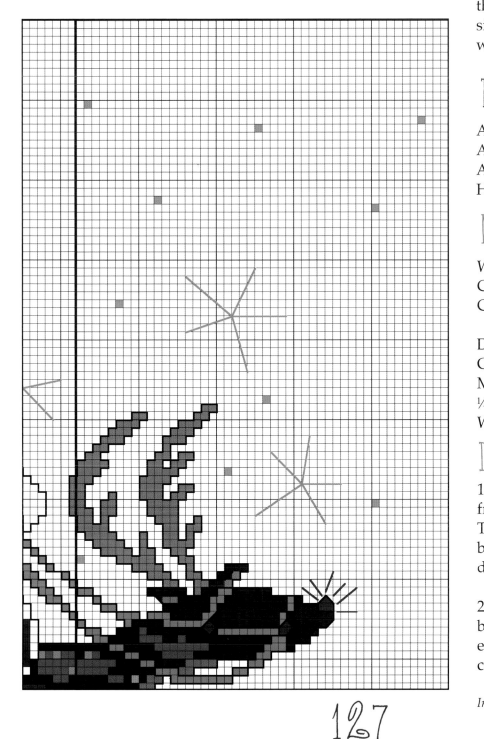

127

Stitched on Hickory Heatherfield 26 over 2 threads, the finished design size is 10⅜" x 11½". The fabric was cut 17" x 18".

Fabrics Design Sizes

Aida 11	12¼" x 13½"
Aida 14	9⅝" x 9⅝"
Aida 18	7½" x 8¼"
Hardanger 22	6⅛" x 6¾"

Materials

Wood frame
Cardstock
Color photocopy of art on
      page 131 at 150%
Decoupage mixture
Gold and black acrylic paint
Matte finish acrylic spray
¼" paintbrush
Wide flat brush

Directions

1. With wide flat brush, paint frame with gold acrylic paint. Two thin coats of paint work better than one thick coat. Let dry completely.

2. Side load ¼" brush with black paint and shade outside edge of frame. Let dry completely.

Instructions Continued on page 129

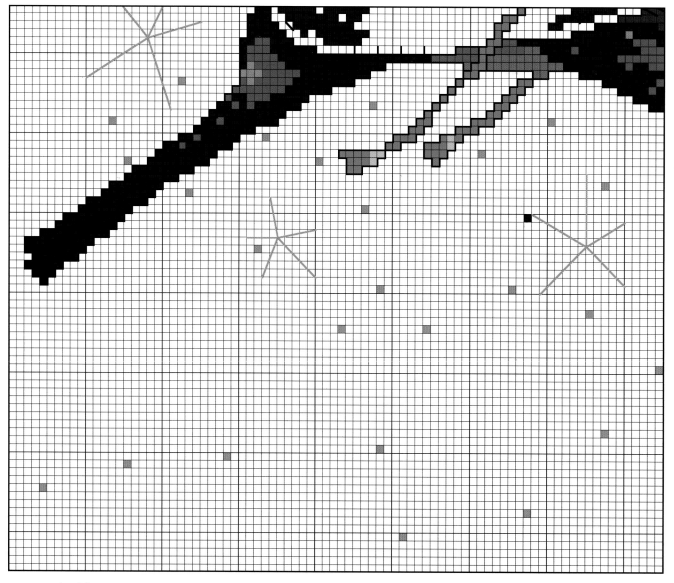

DMC   Anchor

Cross-stitch (2 strands)
☐   White   1
■   742 Tangerine lt.   303
◩ ⌐742 Tangerine lt. (1 strand)   303
     ⌐   Gold balger blending filament (1 strand)
☐   948 Peach vy. dk.   880
◩   3708 Melon lt.   26
■   321 Christmas Red 47
◩   911 Emerald Green med.   205
■   699 Christmas Green 923
◩ ⌐699 Christmas Green (1 strand)   923
     ⌐   Gold balger blending filament (1 strand)
☐   739 Tan ultra vy. lt.   885

■   3773 Pecan vy. lt.   882
■   434 Brown lt.   370
■   301 Mahogany med. 349
■   400 Mahogany dk.   351
■   3024 Brown Gray vy. lt. 900
■   310 Black   403

Backstitch (1 strand)
─   310 Black   403

French Knots (1 strand)
●   310 Black   403

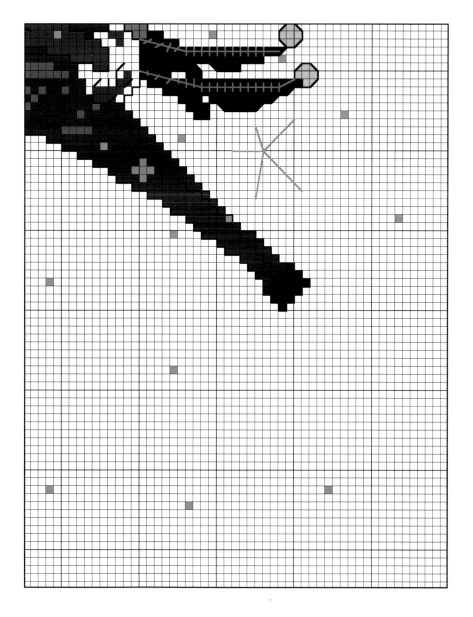

Instructions Continued from Page 127

3. Cut out shapes from color copy of artwork. Following manufacturer's directions, decoupage artwork onto cardstock. Let dry completely. Cut out shapes and decoupage onto frame, using artwork as a guide.

4. Let frame dry completely. Apply one more coat of decoupage mixture to entire frame to seal artwork.

5. Spray several coats of matte finish acrylic spray.

6. Using a fine tip pen, outline artwork. Draw random dots over entire frame to match artwork on page 130.

Beads
60479 Frosted White

Long stitch (2 strands)
— 003 Red Balger blending filament

Ribbon stars
— Golden yellow 4mm silk ribbon

Couched thread (2 strands)
— DMC Silver blending filament

Joyride

To
From:

Treasures
for
the Tree

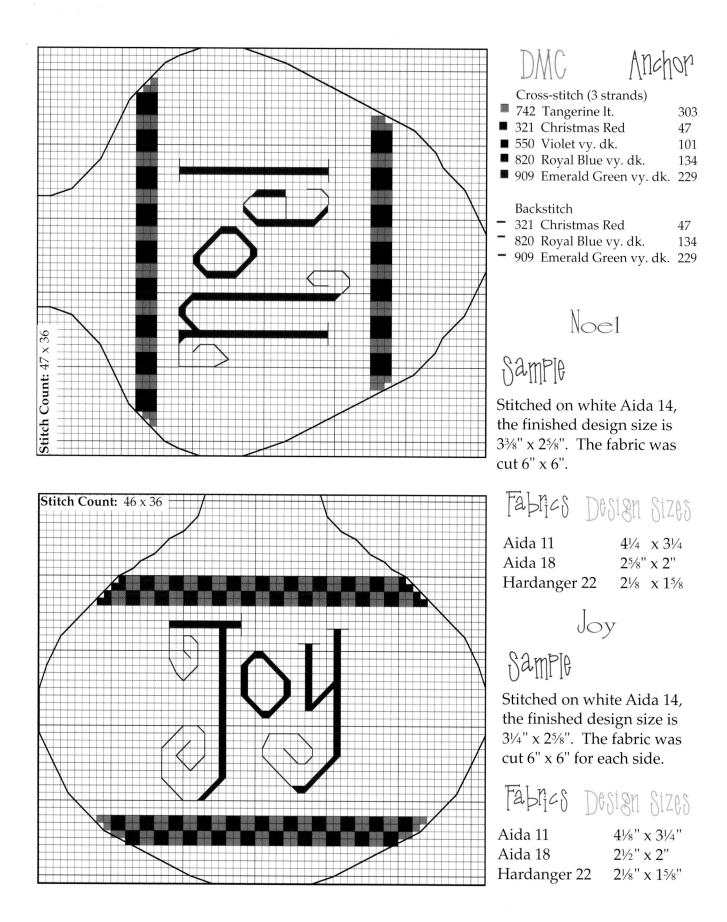

Stitch Count: 47 x 36

Stitch Count: 46 x 36

DMC   **Anchor**

Cross-stitch (3 strands)

	742	Tangerine lt.	303
	321	Christmas Red	47
	550	Violet vy. dk.	101
	820	Royal Blue vy. dk.	134
	909	Emerald Green vy. dk.	229

Backstitch

	321	Christmas Red	47
-	820	Royal Blue vy. dk.	134
-	909	Emerald Green vy. dk.	229

Noel

Sample

Stitched on white Aida 14, the finished design size is 3⅜" x 2⅝". The fabric was cut 6" x 6".

Fabrics   Design Sizes

Aida 11	4¼ x 3¼
Aida 18	2⅝" x 2"
Hardanger 22	2⅛ x 1⅝

Joy

Sample

Stitched on white Aida 14, the finished design size is 3¼" x 2⅝". The fabric was cut 6" x 6" for each side.

Fabrics   Design Sizes

Aida 11	4⅛" x 3¼"
Aida 18	2½" x 2"
Hardanger 22	2⅛" x 1⅝"

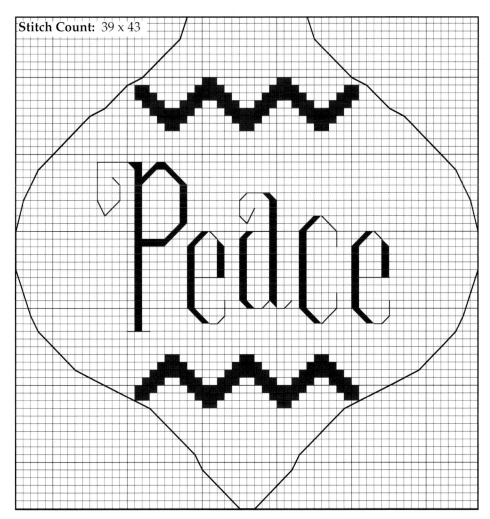

Stitch Count: 39 x 43

Sample

Stitched on white Aida 14, the finished design size is 2¾ " x 3⅛". The fabric was cut 6" x 6".

Fabrics Design Sizes

Aida 11   3½" x 4"
Aida 18   2⅛" x 2⅜"
Hardanger 22   1¾" x 2"

Treasures for the Tree

Materials

Finished designs on white Aida 14 trimmed to 8" squares
Three 8" squares of white Aida 14
Stuffing
3 yards of ¼" wide gold ribbon
4 yards of ⅛" wide red satin ribbon

Directions

1. Pin blank Aida squares on top of cross-stitched squares, right sides together. Using lines on graph, cut out pattern. Stitch around edges with ¼" seam, leaving a 1½" opening. Turn and stuff firmly. Whipstitch opening closed.

2. Cut three 8" pieces of red satin ribbon. Loop and tack to top of each ornament for hanger. Cut remaining red and gold ribbon into three 1 yard pieces. Make a 3-loop bow and tack to top of each ornament.

Playful
Presents

Playful Presents

DMC   Anchor

Cross-stitch (2 strands)

☐	White	1
	3774 Peach Pecan med.	933
	951 Peach Pecan lt.	366
	743 Yellow med.	297
	3716 Wild Rose lt.	50
■	321 Christmas Red	47
■	498 Christmas Red dk.	20
■	553 Violet med.	98
■	912 Emerald Green lt.	204
■	909 Emerald Green vy. dk.	229
	3782 Mocha Brown lt.	899
	3776 Mahogany lt.	338
■	400 Mahogany dk.	351
■	433 Brown med.	371
■	310 Black	403

Backstitch (1 strand)

—	310 Black	403

French knots (1 strand)

•	310 Black	403

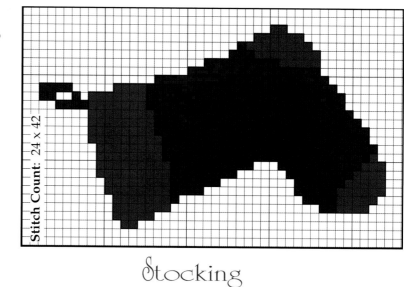

Stitch Count: 24 x 42

Stocking

Sample

Stitched on clear perforated plastic 14, the finished design size was 1¾" x 3". The plastic was cut 5" x 5".

Fabrics Design Sizes

Aida 11	2⅛" x 3⅞"
Aida 18	1⅜" x 2⅜"
Hardanger	1⅛" x 1⅞"

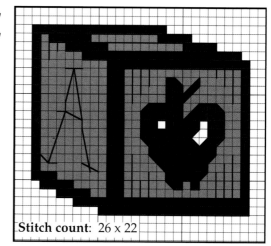

Teddy Bear

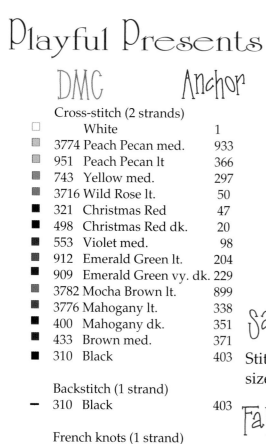

Stitch Count: 28 x 31

Stitch count: 26 x 22

Sample

Stitched on clear perforated plactic 14, the finished design size is 2" x 2¼". The plastic was cut 5" x 5"

Fabrics   Design Sizes

Aida 11	2½" x 2⅞"
Aida 18	1½" x 1¾"
Hardanger 22	1¼" x 1⅜"

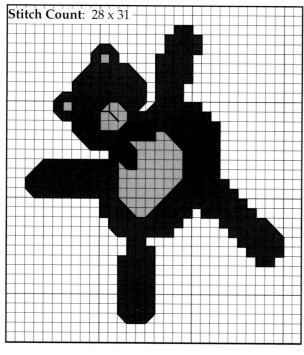

Stitch count: 40 x 67

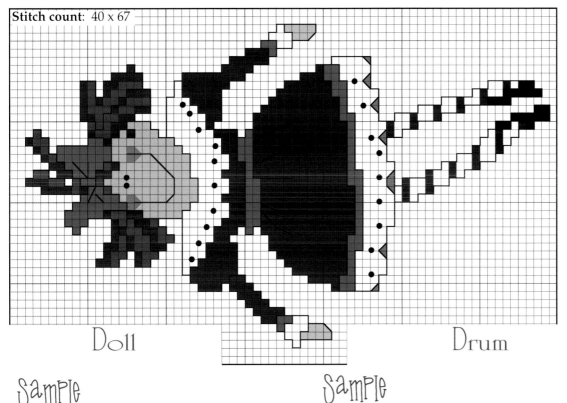

Doll

Drum

Sample

Stitched on clear perforated plastic 14, the finished design size is 2⅞" x 4¾". The plastic was cut 6" x 7".

Fabrics · Design Sizes

Fabrics	Design Sizes
Aida 11	3⅝" x 6⅛"
Aida 18	2¼" x 3¾"
Hardanger 22	1⅞" x 3"

Sample

Stitched on clear perforated plastic 14, the finished design size is 2⅛" x 2". The plastic was cut 5" x 5".

Fabrics · Design Sizes

Fabrics	Design Sizes
Aida 11	2⅝" x 2½"
Aida 18	1⅝" x 1½"
Hardanger 22	1⅜" x 1 ¼"

Block

Sample

Stitched on clear perforated plastic 14 over 1 thread, the finished design size is 1⅞" x 1⅝". The plastic was cut 5" x 5".

Fabrics · Design Sizes

Fabrics	Design Sizes
Aida ll	2⅜" x 2"
Aida 18	1½" x 1¼"
Hardanger 22	1⅛" x 1"

Stitch Count: 29 x 28

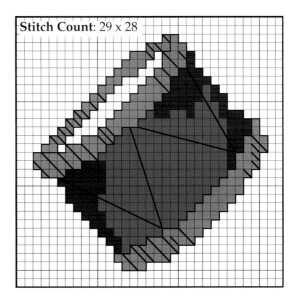

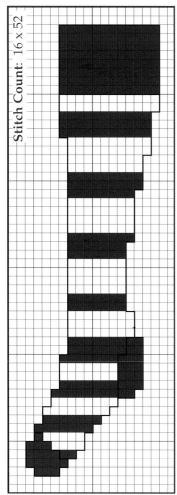

Stitch Count: 16 x 52

Red Stocking

Sample

Stitched on clear perforated plastic 14, the finished design size is 1⅛" x 3¾". The plastic was cut 5" x 6".

Fabrics	Design Sizes
Aida 11	1½" x 4¾"
Aida 18	⅞" x 2⅞"
Hardanger 22	¾" x 2⅜"

Toy Soldier

Sample

Stitched on clear perforated plastic 14, the finished design size is 1¾" x 6¾". The plastic was cut 5" x 9".

Fabrics	Design Sizes
Aida 11	2⅛" x 8½"
Aida 18	1⅜" x 5¼"
Hardanger 22	1⅛" x 4¼"

Top

Sample

Stitched on clear perforated plastic 14, the finished design size is 1⅝" x 2⅛". The plastic was cut 5" x 5".

Fabrics	Design Sizes
Aida 11	2" x 2¾"
Aida 18	1¼" x 1⅝"
Hardanger 22	1" x 1⅜"

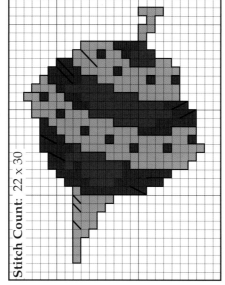

Stitch Count: 22 x 30

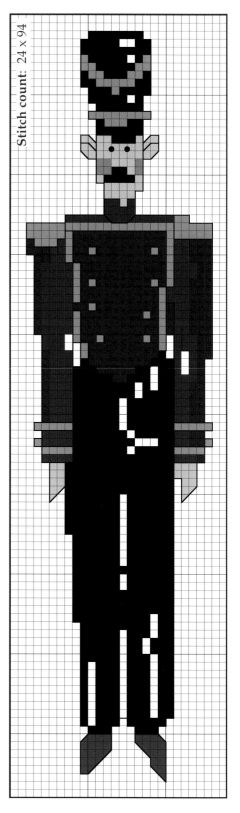

Stitch count: 24 x 94

General Instructions

Cross-stitch Tips

Cross-stitch: Make one cross-stitch for each symbol on chart. Bring needle up at A, down at B, up at C, down at D; see diagram. For rows, stitch across fabric from left to right to make half-crosses and then back to complete stitches.

Fabrics: Designs in this book are worked on even-weave fabrics made especially for cross-stitch, which can be found in most needlework shops. Fabrics used for models are identified in sample informations by color, name, and thread count per inch.

Preparing fabric: Cut fabric at least 3" larger on all sides than finished design size or cut as indicated in sample information to ensure enough space for project assembly. To keep fabric from fraying, whipstitch or machine-zigzag along raw edges or apply liquid ravel preventer.

Needles: Choose needle that will slip easily through fabric holes without piercing fabric threads. For fabric with 11 or fewer threads per inch, use needle size 24; for 14 threads per inch, use needle size 24 or 26; for 18 or more threads per inch, use needle size 26. Never leave needle in design area of fabric. It may leave rust or permanent impression on fabric.

Finished design size: To determine size of finished design, divide stitch count by number of threads per inch of fabric. When design is stitched over two threads, divide stitch count by half the threads per inch.

Floss: Use 18" lengths of floss. For best coverage, separate strands. Dampen with wet sponge. Then put back together number of strands called for in color code.

Stitching method: For smooth stitches, use push-and-pull method. Starting on wrong side of fabric, bring needle straight up, pulling floss completely through to right side. Reinsert needle and bring it back straight down, pulling needle and floss completely through to back of fabric. Keep floss flat, but do not pull thread tight. For even stitches, tension should be consistent throughout.

Beadwork: To attach beads to fabric, bring needle up at A, through bead and down at B (lower left to upper right). Secure, bringing needle up at C, through bead and down at D (lower right to upper left).

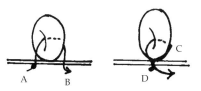

French knots: Bring needle up at A. Wrap floss around needle two times. Insert needle beside A, pulling floss until it fits snugly around needle. Pull needle through to back.

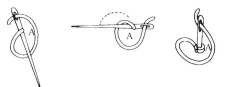

Metric Equivalency Chart

MM-Millimetres   CM-Centimetres
INCHES TO MILLIMETRES AND CENTIMETRES

INCHES	MM	CM	INCHES	CM	INCHES	CM
⅛	3	0.3	9	22.9	30	76.2
¼	6	0.6	10	25.4	31	78.7
½	13	1.3	12	30.5	33	83.8
⅝	16	1.6	13	33.0	34	86.4
¾	19	1.9	14	35.6	35	88.9
⅞	22	2.2	15	38.1	36	91.4
1	25	2.5	16	40.6	37	94.0
1¼	32	3.2	17	43.2	38	96.5
1½	38	3.8	18	45.7	39	99.1
1¾	44	4.4	19	48.3	40	101.6
2	51	5.1	20	50.8	41	104.1
2½	64	6.4	21	53.3	42	106.7
3	76	7.6	22	55.9	43	109.2
3½	89	8.9	23	58.4	44	111.8
4	102	10.2	24	61.0	45	114.3
4½	114	11.4	25	63.5	46	116.8
5	127	12.7	26	66.0	47	119.4
6	152	15.2	27	68.6	48	121.9
7	178	17.8	28	71.1	49	124.5
8	203	20.3	29	73.7	50	127.0

YARDS TO METRES

YARDS	METRES	YARDS	METRES	YARDS	METRES	YARDS	METRES	YARDS	METRES
⅛	0.11	2⅛	1.94	4⅛	3.77	6⅛	5.60	8⅛	7.43
¼	0.23	2¼	2.06	4¼	3.89	6¼	5.72	8¼	7.54
⅜	0.34	2⅜	2.17	4⅜	4.00	6⅜	5.83	8⅜	7.66
½	0.46	2½	2.29	4½	4.11	6½	5.94	8½	7.77
⅝	0.57	2⅝	2.40	4⅝	4.23	6⅝	6.06	8⅝	7.89
¾	0.69	2¾	2.51	4¾	4.34	6¾	6.17	8¾	8.00
⅞	0.80	2⅞	2.63	4⅞	4.46	6⅞	6.29	8⅞	8.12
1	0.91	3	2.74	5	4.57	7	6.40	9	8.23
1⅛	1.03	3⅛	2.86	5⅛	4.69	7⅛	6.52	9⅛	8.34
1¼	1.14	3¼	2.97	5¼	4.80	7¼	6.63	9¼	8.46
1⅜	1.26	3⅜	3.09	5⅜	4.91	7⅜	6.74	9⅜	8.57
1½	1.37	3½	3.20	5½	5.03	7½	6.86	9½	8.69
1⅝	1.49	3⅝	3.31	5⅝	5.14	7⅝	6.97	9⅝	8.80
1¾	1.60	3¾	3.43	5¾	5.26	7¾	7.09	9¾	8.92
1⅞	1.71	3⅞	3.54	5⅞	5.37	7⅞	7.20	9⅞	9.03
2	1.83	4	3.66	6	5.49	8	7.32	10	9.14

Index